the other side of the gun

SUSAN SNOW

the other side of the gun

My Journey from Trauma to Resiliency

Legacy Press

The Other Side of the Gun: My Journey from Trauma to Resiliency
Susan Snow
Copyright ©2023 by Susan Snow

Paperback ISBN: 979-8-9873294-0-5
Ebook ISBN: 979-8-9873294-1-2
Library of Congress Control Number: 2023900491

Legacy Press

Legacy Press LLC
Castle Rock, Colorado
SusanSnowSpeaks.com

Editing by Melanie Mulhall, Dragonheart, The Dragonheart.com
Cover and interior design by YellowStudios, YellowStudiosOnline.com
Cover artwork by Dylan Snow
Back cover photo by Shreffler Photography

First Edition
Printed in the United States of America

Note to the reader: Some names have been changed to protect the privacy of those involved.

Contents

Foreword

It was one of those warm idyllic summer days in August of 1985 when I first met the family of Tom Williams, a detective with the Los Angeles Police Department. I was also a detective with the same department, assigned to Robbery-Homicide Division's Major Crimes Unit.

I did not know Tom before running into him and his family at the restaurant of the Catamaran Hotel on Mission Bay in San Diego. I was there with my family, and we had gone to breakfast before a day of playing on the adjacent beach with the catamaran and sailboards I brought on our vacation. I looked over at the family dining in one of the nearby booths and recognized Tom as a fellow officer on the job, even though we didn't really know each other. I went over, introduced myself, and invited them to join us on the beach that day.

We sailed the bay on the catamaran, and I taught Susan and Ryan, Tom's children, the fundamentals of sailboarding. I guess I wasn't the best of instructors because we had to rescue

Susan when she drifted a considerable distance from the beach trying to maneuver the somewhat tricky craft. But all things considered, it was a fun day with our newfound friends.

Fast-forward nearly three months to Halloween, October 31, 1985. I was just heading home after the normal workday had ended when I received a notification that an off-duty officer had been shot and killed at a church school in Canoga Park. It was my assigned unit's responsibility to handle the investigation of any law enforcement officer murdered in the line of duty in the City of Angels, and it was to my utter dismay as I arrived at the crime scene to recognize the victim of the shooting as none other than Detective Tom Williams.

I learned that he had been picking up his six-year-old son Ryan at the church school he attended. Ryan was on the passenger side inside his dad's pickup truck when the fatal shots were fired from a fully automatic weapon. As the investigation unfolded, I was assigned as the lead detective on Tom's case.

Thus began the three-year odyssey of investigation and court proceedings in two trials for the various defendants involved in the conspiracy to murder Detective Williams. It was a unique case in the annals of LAPD history to have an officer targeted to be murdered for just doing his job.

As is inherent in any investigation of this nature, the assigned detective becomes very close to the victim's family, and we have remained so to this day, thirty-seven years later. I am honored to have been asked by Susan to provide a brief introduction to the tale you are about to read concerning the personal impact the incident has wrought upon her, her brother Ryan, and her mom Norma. I'm certain you will be deeply moved by Susan's story.

Mike Thies, Detective III, LAPD (1964-1989),
retired November 2022

Part 1
My Story

1

The Night
That Changed My Life

Mom looked tired as she came in through the back door, still wearing her Halloween Tin Man costume. Remnants of silvery makeup lingered on her face. The sun was starting to set and the temperature was falling by the time she got home that Halloween night in 1985. Mom's company had a contest for the best Halloween costume, and she had wanted to win. She told me about the contest and all the drama of the day, and then she adjourned to the kitchen.

I answered the phone when it rang, and a woman from my brother's school was on the other end of the line. Her voice was shaky as she told me there had been a drive by shooting and my dad was involved. My mom came around the corner from the kitchen and I quickly handed her the phone. Something didn't feel right, and my legs gave out.

As my mom listened to the woman speak, she wiped the remainder of her makeup off. I watched her face turn pale and her posture start to slump. When she hung up the call, she frantically said, "Susan get in the van. We're going to Faith Baptist School."

The ten minutes it took to get to the school felt like forever, and the emptiness in the pit of my stomach grew the closer we got to the school. When we got to the school and parked the car, my mom almost forgot to pull the keys out of the ignition as she jumped out. The night sky was lit up by the ambulance lights, but it sat motionless, and when the police officers on the scene saw who was approaching, there were tears in their eyes but their gaze was hollow.

As we rounded the ambulance, Mom spotted my dad's truck, and we both ran toward it. Shattered glass was all over the street and the truck was riddled with bullets. My dad was slumped against the truck with a white rumpled sheet slightly covering him. I could see a sliver of his body peeking out from under the sheet and a little bit of his hair blowing in the wind. When police officers grabbed my mom's arm to hold her back, her legs buckled and she almost lost her balance.

"No! Please, no!" she screamed. She kept bellowing that until she realized my little brother Ryan was nowhere around.

I stood there in total disbelief. I wondered why no one was helping my dad and I wondered where Ryan was. My dad had been at the school to pick him up. Was Ryan hurt? Had he seen what happened? The thought of what he might have seen terrified me.

One of the school administrators and a police officer met us as we found our way back to the small parking lot. As we followed them to the school office, my eyes were focused on the other people weeping. Somehow, I still did not understand. It felt like my brain was stuck and I couldn't move forward.

I heard two women speaking in the office. One woman said, "Tragically, Detective Williams was killed tonight. Someone drove by and shot him."

Suddenly, it became real as her words pierced me and sent chills down my spine. It felt like every nerve in my body was about to explode. *God, please wake me up from this nightmare,* I thought. I felt a deep need to run as fast as my legs would go, but my legs felt heavy and I couldn't muster any strength. I just stood there in the office, yearning to hear my dad's voice.

My world collapsed, and I didn't want to be there anymore. I began to sob uncontrollably.

My mom entered the room and said, "You can't go home. I'm going to call Toni to come get you. You'll stay with them."

Our neighbor, Toni, came and took me to her house, but I was too much in shock to even know what was happening until we got to her door. Toni grabbed me and tried to console me as I wept into her shoulder. My heart pounded through my chest and I couldn't breathe. I felt helpless. I just wanted to reboot, start over, and leave the deep, dark pit that now lived in my soul.

Toni tried everything to calm me, but it didn't work. I knew she was talking to me, but I couldn't hear her. All I could hear was the droning in my head. I was at a loss for words. All

I wanted was my boyfriend Matt. "Please call Matt," I pleaded. "He's working, but I need him."

I told her where he worked, and she reached him by phone, telling him we had an emergency with my dad but providing no other details. It felt like an eternity before he arrived at Toni's house. With his keys dangling from his hand, I saw the look of worry in his eyes as he said, "Grab your coat. I'm taking you to the hospital."

I stood at the door unable to speak and he kept demanding me to come with him. Finally, I took a breath. "He's not there. He's gone," I said.

The look on Matt's face changed, and I could see the despair enveloping him. Tears welled up in his eyes as he dropped to his knees. With my help, Matt stood up, entered the house, and pulled me into his embrace. I never wanted to let him go in that moment. I simply melted into his arms and sobbed. I knew he wanted to know what happened, but he just held me until I was able to be calm.

Later that night, Matt walked me down the street to my house. We both noticed police cruisers going up and down my street, and my driveway was filled with cars I didn't recognize. Uniformed officers were on the front lawn. They'd been walking about since it was dark. Shadows of them walking were being created by their flashlights, and a couple of the officers aimed their flashlights at Matt and me. From behind me a voice said, "It's his daughter." As we got closer, I saw his ashen face. "I'm so sorry," he said.

Matt and I made our way to my porch, and Matt slowly opened the door. We were met with at least twenty people standing around my living room and the smell of fresh coffee coming from the kitchen. I could hear my mom's voice talking to someone through the noise of the conversations around us. Feeling like a stranger in my own house, I wondered who all the people were.

Matt and I walked down the hallway, hoping to avoid getting stopped by anyone. I just wanted to crawl into my bed and put the covers over my head. I had no more energy. We made it to my room without anyone talking to us. As we sat on my twin bed, I could hear footsteps and chatter in the living room, but we sat in silence with Matt sweetly holding my hand. The weight of the night was heavy, and all we could do was lie down, huddled on my bed together.

As Matt was lying next to me, I looked over to see that his eyes were starting to close and one tear rolled down his left temple. "Matt, you can go home if you want," I said quietly in his ear.

He sat up and wiped the wetness from his eyes. "Stay in bed," he replied. "I'll be back tomorrow." He leaned over and kissed my forehead.

I couldn't even muster up the energy to lift my head off the pillow.

Matt left the room and quietly closed the door. Faintly, I heard someone talking to him in the hallway. I sank down further into the bed as I listened to the many conversations going on inside my house all night.

When the sunlight caught my eye as it gleamed through my window blind, I knew it was now morning. I had been awake all night. Still barely able to function, I sat up and rose to my feet. My legs felt like lead as I slowly opened my door and quietly crept down to my bathroom. Still feeling like the night was just a nightmare, I glanced out the bathroom window to see uniformed officers walking around in front of our house and the same cars in the driveway. I realized that this was reality—my reality.

Instead of dad's orange and black Toyota pickup truck in our driveway, there were armed police officers in front of the house wearing black bands across their badges. There were officers in the backyard too, police helicopters circling the neighborhood overhead, and police cars lining the street of my once quiet neighborhood.

Mom was so busy talking to the victim advocates that I barely had a conversation with her. I finally saw Ryan come out of his room. I'd thought I heard him crying during the night but didn't have the energy to check on him and felt bad about that. I'd figured my mom would calm him.

My teenage mind had difficulty taking it all in. I asked myself how I was going to get my old life back, but at some level I knew that everything had profoundly changed and there was no going back to that life.

Dad and Ryan in soccer

Madonna and Billy idol

Me, dad and brother

2

My Dad the Protector

My father and I had been very close. I couldn't imagine life without him.

As a police detective, he had an intensity of concentration I'd never seen in any other person. It was as though his consciousness transported him to a different world when he set his mind on solving a crime. He would sit in our den with his yellow notepads, reports, and photos spread out neatly on his big desk and just stare. His mind made connections in the scraps of details. He made order out of confusion and found patterns in the chaos as he analyzed the effects of human depravity and crime.

My mom would occasionally offer him some coffee or water, to which he would raise his head and smile as he politely accepted it. Then he would lower his head to again study the papers before him. My little brother and I would occasionally glance through the door, but we knew not to interrupt.

He'd brought the same kind of focus to ordinary family things too. Once, he'd reluctantly agreed to coach my little brother's soccer team because the regular coach had become ill. He knew nothing about soccer. He tried to bury his dread about not knowing or understanding the subtleties of the game, but it was obvious to Mom and me. He'd buried himself in a tattered, highlighted book about soccer rules because he was not about to embarrass his son by not being prepared. He even brought the book to the kitchen table, and his look of determination made me giggle. As he sat there, he unconsciously pulled on his nose just as he did when he was in deep thought about a case at work.

My father was also the arbiter of right behavior for both my brother and me. When he confronted me after learning that a girlfriend and I had been smoking cigarettes, he had a look on his face I'd never seen before and a vein at the side of his temple was bulging. He presented the evidence and I tried to deny any knowledge of the cigarette butts. But he was a police detective, so there was no way I was going to get out of the situation with a denial. Besides, my little brother had seen my friend and me in the act and had reported it to my father.

Once I retreated to my bedroom, after hearing from my father that he was disappointed in me and receiving the punishment of being grounded for two weeks, I contemplated his disappointment. The last thing I wanted to do was disappoint my dad. A while later, he came into my room and sat down on the bed next to me. The vein in his temple was no longer swollen, but he looked worried. He pulled me close to him and put his arm around me. Then he began telling me stories about kids who grew up too fast, made bad choices, and had bad endings.

"Susie, I love you," he said. "I don't ever want anything bad to happen to you, and I hope I can teach you to make better choices as you grow up."

I listened to him that night. But the listening wasn't just one-way in our relationship. It was reciprocal. He listened to me too, something I struggled with in my relationship with my mother.

Dad was not only my protector when it came to helping me make good choices, he was my protector when it came to potential danger in the world. One day when I was fourteen or fifteen, a man pulled up along the side of the busy street I was on as I walked home from school. He kept calling out to me to get my attention, waving a piece of paper and asking for directions. This was one of the situations my dad had warned me about, and it felt as if he were sitting on my shoulder, telling me to stay safely away from the car.

I made a decision in the moment to get close enough to see the paper but not so close that he could grab me. As I approached, he began saying vulgar things to me and I saw that his hands were down his pants. I panicked and began running, but I wasn't so panicked that I neglected to hear my dad's voice in my head. *Don't go home. Go to the neighbor's house.*

Once safely at the neighbor's house, I called my dad at work and told him what had happened. When he came for me after work, he said, "Susie, you did the right thing by going straight to Toni's house." Then he said we were going to get in his car and drive around to see if we could identify the make and model of the car. I knew he was serious because that vein on his temple was bulging. This time, though, his anger wasn't aimed at me but at the man who intended to hurt me. He was determined to find him.

"Tomorrow we're going to the Parker Center to work with a sketch artist to describe this man so we can get a sketch of him."

I was embarrassed about the whole situation and would have preferred to avoid having to describe the situation again and go into detail about the man's appearance. "Wow, Dad," I said. "Can't we just forget about what happened?"

But my father the protector was not going to do that. Once the sketch had been drawn the next day, my father took it, handed it to a police officer, and told him to put out an alert for the guy. The man was never found, but I was secure in the knowledge that my father's advice about how to deal with potentially dangerous situations had sunk in enough for me to act spontaneously exactly as I should when I encountered one. And I knew he would do everything in his power to protect both me and anyone else from being harmed by people who intended to hurt us.

That protection extended to my dating life. I met Matt—the man who would later become my husband and the boy I was dating when my father died—when I went to a park with some friends. My friend Wendi had been talking about a college guy she was dating for weeks, and I was finally going to meet the elusive boy named Matt. I was immediately drawn to him, but I knew he was off-limits because he was Wendi's boyfriend. I tried to play it cool, but when we were introduced and he looked right into my eyes, I felt butterflies fluttering in my stomach. Still, I followed the girl code: You didn't flirt with another girl's guy. Even so, every once in a while, I saw him glance my way.

A couple of weeks later, Wendi told me she'd met someone she really liked. Matt was out of the picture. That made him no longer off-limits. I saw him again in a group setting at the park one night, so talking with him was easy. But it was more than that. I felt a level of comfort talking with him that I'd never felt with any other guy. When my friends and I were about to leave the park that night, he hugged me tightly, and I felt the energy between us.

My dad the protector came to my room one night a couple of weeks later with a look of confusion on his face and nervously said, "You have a phone call."

It was Matt, and he asked if he could come by and see me.

"A guy friend is coming over to see me," I told my parents when we hung up. "He won't stay too late. I promise."

"Who is this guy?" Dad asked.

"He's a friend, and he's really nice," I replied.

When he arrived, he followed me into the living room to meet my mom and dad. The well-mannered Matt shook hands with them, and both of my parents struck up a conversation with him. When I saw that my father was taking over the conversation with my date, I suggested to Matt that we talk outside on our front porch.

Matt and I talked on the phone every chance we could. Besides going to college, he worked a lot. Matt was nineteen at the time, and my dad had told me I could only date boys my own age. Fortunately, Matt had a baby face and looked younger than he was.

That summer, I went to summer school because my algebra grade had been low. Before summer school started, my father had a conversation with me. "Susie, for you to continue seeing Matt, you need to earn a C grade or better in algebra."

That was all the motivation I needed. I passed with a C. Matt and I celebrated with a trip to the beach, and that night, he took me to dinner and a movie. And later, after a movie we barely saw because we kissed most of the way through it, he took me on a carriage ride and presented me with a rose. Wrapped together in blankets on our ride, I felt safe and warm in his arms.

And as the months progressed, Matt and my parents forged a good relationship. My dad really liked him and frequently commented that he was glad I'd found a nice boy to date. That nice boy who had made me feel safe and warm in his arms was to become my rock. I'd always known I could count on my dad's leadership, his guidance, his wisdom, his love, and his protection. But now my protector was gone.

3

Preparing to Say Good-Bye

Sleep continued to elude me before the funeral. I knew I had to say good-bye to my hero, and I knew I had to find something appropriate to wear at the funeral to do that. But I felt unmotivated and in a haze.

A family friend picked me up, and along with that person, I walked into the mall with two plain clothes police officers in tow. Life had gotten complicated. It was believed that my mother, brother, and I might also be in danger too, so I was now a teenager who had bodyguards to do the simple task of shopping for clothes.

The mall was a place I normally would love to spend time, but this time it felt like a chore. Trudging through the many stores, I kept putting one foot in front of the other. I dragged myself through the clothing racks, but I just couldn't find the perfect outfit.

Out of my fog, I heard our friend's voice. "Susan, you need to find an outfit for your dad's service." Tears were streaming down my face as she said, "Pick out something your dad would like."

Hanging on a rack in front of me was the perfect suit in a dark shade of blue and embossed with black flowers—the colors of law enforcement.

Back at home, I went straight into my room. The experience at the mall had been taxing, so I lay down on my bed. I started to think about my dad and all the times he'd given me life lessons. I yearned for him to tell me how I was supposed to live without him. I missed him every minute of the day and I wanted to hear his deep, strong voice. I missed the smell of his pipe smoke, and I realized I would have even loved to hear him snore as he slept.

I wondered if he would like the outfit I picked out for his funeral, and I thought about the morning he died, the last morning I'd been able to spend time with him. It was not a normal morning for him. He had a look of distress on his face. "I can't figure out the right tie to go with my suit," he'd said to me. "Your mom has already left for the day. Can you help me, Susie?"

Dad was a little color blind and had little fashion sense, so I agreed to help him out. I'd hoped he would let me go to a friend's party that night because I'd helped him pick out the tie. I knew it was a little manipulative, but I was desperate. I saw a little bit of sweat beading on his forehead when he nervously laid out the ties on his bed. As I held up each one to his shirt, the vein in his temple showed his stress. "Here you go, Dad," I said. "Put this one on. It will look great!" Then, as I started to walk away, I turned back to him and said, "Dad, can I go to a party tonight with Matt?"

"Susie it's a school night and I don't think I want you out late," he replied. "It's time for school. Go get your stuff."

I grabbed my backpack, stuffed my makeup inside, ran out to his truck, and jumped in the passenger seat.

With a look of disappointment on his face, he'd said, "Susan, please take off all of that makeup. You're beautiful without it."

I took a crumpled up tissue from his hand and wiped off my lipstick and blush. "Just drop me off across the street from school, Dad. I'm meeting a friend, and we can walk from there."

"Okay," he said. He pulled over, and as I got out of the truck, he leaned over and said, "Go ahead. And you can wear a little makeup. Have a good day, honey. I'll see you tonight. We'll take Ryan trick or treating."

I waved good-bye as he drove off, but I felt frustrated with our conversation. The whole day at school, I kept hoping he would have a change of heart and give me permission to go to the party. When the school bell rang at 3:00 p.m., I headed out of the door of my school building and waved to my friends. "See you later!" I said, hoping it would be true. I started my long walk home thinking about putting my Halloween costume together once I got there.

From the minute I came through the front door, I frantically started to tear through the house, cleaning everything in sight. I was doing everything I could to impress my parents so they would see my efforts and grant me permission to go to the party.

Permission didn't happen. Instead, we received the call that brought my life crashing down and broke it into tiny pieces. Even the good times I had prior to that night were shattered.

4

The Funeral

Laying out my suit across my crumpled up comforter, I recalled that conversation with my dad the morning he died. I felt guilty because it was the last conversation I had with him before he died. I couldn't apologize to him, and that hurt me to my core.

I got dressed and wiped the tears from my face. The black stretch limousine was waiting for us. Matt stood at the back of the limo waiting for me, and ahead of the limo was a line of about thirty motor cops on our side of the street. Matt held the door for me as I entered the limo. My mom and Ryan were already sitting to the front. Ryan looked so forlorn on that deep leather seat with his little hands in his lap, and tears welled up in my eyes. Matt immediately grabbed my hand and began gently stroking it with his fingertips. Just that small gesture made me relax a little.

As we started our journey down the street, I looked out of the window to see neighbors standing on the street, waving to us as we drove past. The church was located on Topanga Canyon, a very busy boulevard, and as we turned onto the street, Matt leaned over to me and told me to look. Members of our community were lining the street on both sides, saluting and waving flags. I started to feel my head spin as I wondered if it was all for my dad.

Approaching the church with the blue and red lights flashing from the motorcade, I looked out of the window to see rows and rows of police officers standing at attention. Police cars with the lights blaring could be seen farther than my eyes could focus. All of the officers wore black bands stretched across their shiny badges.

When we stepped out of the limousine and started our walk to the church entrance, I kept my head down so all I saw was the freshly polished boots of the officers we passed. I finally looked up and saw that tears were silently streaming down their faces. That silence was deafening. As I caught their gaze, my legs started to tremble. It all felt surreal to me, like an out of body experience. My heart was in deep despair.

Flowers were in beautiful arrangements at the front of the sanctuary, and as we entered, their smell permeated the air. My heart was pounding as I walked up the aisle, and I kept my focus on the large mural of Jesus ahead. We found our seats and Matt and I sat next to my mom, Ryan, my dad's best friend Roger, and my dad's mom. The wood on the pews felt cold and hard as I sat there in a haze. All I could do was look up and notice the sun shining through the stained glass windows on both sides of the sanctuary.

I sat there feeling angry with God. I'd spent many weekends at that church with my parents, and now I felt betrayed. The priest welcomed everyone, but my brain was really struggling to make sense of the words.

When the priest finished, Police Chief Darryl Gates came to the podium dressed in his blues. He called my dad the policeman's policeman, a by-the-book kind of cop and a hero to many. He spoke of his admiration for all my dad had accomplished in his thirteen-year career. He pontificated about the bravery he showed when he saved my brother's life that Halloween night. With the quick reflexes of the career law enforcement officer he was, my dad had seen the impending danger and yelled at Ryan to duck down when the shooting started. No doubt Ryan was alive because of his quick action. I tried to take in all the accolades my dad was receiving, but all I felt was heartbreak.

Dad's best friend Roger was next at the podium. He stood tall and rigid as he told many funny stories of their younger lives together. As rigid as he was, I could tell he was trying to hold back the tears. His face started to flush as he told us of his anger and sadness at losing his best friend. He spoke of the world losing a good man. He spoke of the love he saw my dad have for his family and how two of the best days of my dad's life were the births of his children.

As I heard the stories about my dad, I expected him to walk in the church and say, "See, everyone. I'm still here." But that didn't happen. Instead I stared at the flag-draped coffin and smelled the incense burning. I could see the media set up out of the corner of my eye, and I felt the camera zeroing in on us just to get the right shot of our pain. I wanted to bury my head in Matt's shoulder and cry to make it all go away, but I didn't. I was my father's daughter, and we were surrounded by dignitaries, friends, family, and media. I needed to stoically get through it.

After the service was over, we followed my dad's coffin up the aisle with the altar boys and priests. Traveling slowly, Matt held my hand and I kept my head down, concentrating on the grey carpet under my feet. Many friends approached us to offer condolences, but I couldn't bring my head up to catch their eyes. Some people waited for us to get closer so they could reach out and hug me. Some had no words, just tears. I could feel their pain.

When we passed through the large wooden doors, we were met with the smell of the hibiscus. We stopped long enough to see the pall bearers place my dad's coffin in the back of the hearse. With one last salute, they backed away slowly. As I entered the limo, I saw my mom consoling Ryan and wondered if she understood my pain too. My eyes squinted as I looked out into the bright blue sky and felt the warm sunshine on my face. I wondered how Earth kept revolving around its axis when I'd lost my dad. It was a beautiful day for him, and I decided my dad must have ordered it to be that way.

The limo driver started the engine and I could see the lights of the motorcade as we made our way back onto Topanga Canyon, headed East toward the 118 Freeway. Again, I could see people lined up on either side of the street. As we approached the on ramp to the highway, we were close to a canyon hikers and teens frequented and that my dad and I had hiked. Matt told me to look up. On the tallest peak of one of the canyon cliffs stood two hikers holding up flags and saluting.

The 118 freeway would take us to San Fernando Mission Cemetery, my dad's final resting place. As we approached the front gate, I saw that the cemetery roads were filled with black-and-white police cars. It felt unreal. I exited the limo with Matt's help. He grabbed my hand and we started to walk when Matt saw that my grandmother was walking alone. He told me he wanted to escort her, so he went to her, took her arm under his, and walked her to where the seats were set up for us. My mom was being escorted by someone from LAPD with Roger and Ryan trailing behind them.

I felt alone in that moment. Roger saw me struggling and came over to me and grabbed my hand. Together we walked to the chairs set up near the casket. I couldn't look at the coffin at his final resting place. It hit me pretty hard at that moment. He was in there and he was not coming back. I wondered how I was going to manage life without him.

The honor guard, made up of representatives from many law enforcement departments, marched through the grass to the front by the casket and stood at attention, holding their flags with pride. From the back, echoing through the cemetery, I heard the first notes of the Los Angeles Police Department bagpipers. They played a marching song until they made their way up to the front and then shifted to "Amazing Grace," which sent shivers down my spine. I held my breath for a moment and began to tremble as tears welled up in my eyes and streamed down my face. I couldn't hold back the tears any longer.

The music stopped playing and the honor guards removed the American flag from my dad's coffin and carefully began the ceremonial folding of it. When they finished, they saluted and presented the flag to Chief Gates. I began to shake. He approached my brother and me and slowly lowered himself to one knee. Gently, he placed the folded flag in Ryan's little hands. Then he leaned toward me. I'm sure he could see that I was barely maintaining my composure. He grabbed my hands and placed a replica of my dad's badge in a tiny jewelry box into my trembling hands.

"Susan, your dad was a hero and you should be very proud," he said. Then he turned to my mom who was seated next to me. "LAPD family is family, and we will always be there for our family." Then he rose to his feet and backed away.

My hands felt sweaty as they held on to the little box, and I continued to struggle with keeping composed.

The gun salute shots rang out, and I felt Ryan shudder next to me. I looked over at him and saw tears streaming down his face. In that moment, I wanted to hold him and tell him that everything was going to be okay, but both of us kept our places, trying to be as stoic as possible.

Four helicopters flew directly over us and one broke away from the rest and flew off into the distance. I felt like the helicopter that broke from the rest, surrounded by so many people who loved me but feeling all alone.

Something deep within told me to look up and around. As I did, I saw all the people my dad had impacted and pride filled my soul as I took inventory of them standing and honoring him that day.

Casket at Church

Squad cars

Burial site

5

Numbing the Pain

After the funeral was over and we were back at the house, I went into my room and collapsed on my bed. In the privacy of my room, I allowed myself to break down. I could let the tears flow without worrying about who was watching me, and that gave me a sense of freedom. I let my mind wander to some of the memories I had of my dad.

The memories of the past hurt, and I felt alone in my pain. I couldn't believe that I would never have my dad there again to give me advice or even to argue with. In my aloneness and pain, I had nothing but memories and thoughts swirling around in my head. I felt frustrated because I wanted to share memories with my mom, but I feared doing so would be painful for her and make her miss him more. I really felt stuck between my current reality and my past reality.

The real reality became clear the morning after the funeral when I walked out of my room toward the sound of the television in the living room. The news was on and they were replaying the coverage of my dad's funeral. I sat there watching, and when the next story came up, the anchor reported that the men suspected of involvement in the murder had been caught. Tears welled up in my puffy eyes as I listened to the details of their arrests. Shots of the scene and of my dad's bullet ridden truck came next. I couldn't take much more.

I got up and went to my bathroom. I hadn't yet looked outside that morning, so I looked out my bathroom window to see if the police presence was still in the front yard. They were gone. I could faintly hear one officer at the front door telling someone that the detail had been called off because the suspects were in custody and we were no longer in danger.

The next couple of weeks were filled with days of haziness. My mom started drinking, and there were days when I couldn't talk to her because she just wanted to be left alone. Ryan went back to school, but I still wasn't ready. The tension in the house was unavoidable, and it just made me miss my dad even more. Mom and I were struggling, and I was just a teenage girl who had no clue how to navigate through the pain.

Matt came over frequently, and he was the only one who could make me feel better. Matt and I would go on walks in the neighborhood, hand in hand, just to talk.

"I feel like I need to be there for my mom and Ryan," I said. "I just don't know how to. I'm really struggling with being angry and sad at the same time. Mom is drinking again. I don't know how to handle it because the last time she drank like this, my dad was here to help her stop. Now he's gone. What do I do now?"

"What do you mean by *again*?" Matt asked, confused.

I had never talked about my foster sister Ginny or Mom's drinking, so I told him the story.

I went on to tell him about the time that mom worked as a social worker at a women's convent. She had made friends with a couple of girls, and one of them was named Virginia. "She called her Ginny for short," I explained. "Ginny was a gorgeous, statuesque teenage girl with long blonde hair and the bluest eyes you've ever seen. Men fell all over themselves around her, which is why she found herself in the convent. She had been sexually abused as a kid, and that caused her to lash out and get in trouble." I paused and he squeezed my hand to let me know it was okay and he wanted me to continue.

"Mom would come home and tell Dad and I stories about the funny things the girls did. Ginny was one of her favorites. Mom's relationship with Ginny began to grow. When she came home from work one day, I could see she was upset. She told my dad that Ginny had been transferred out of the convent to another home for girls and she'd received a call from Ginny. Ginny said the place wasn't safe and she was scared.

"Mom and Dad continued to talk about Ginny until one day they sat me down and told me that we were going to foster her at our house. I was excited because I would finally have a sibling. I was only nine then, and I couldn't wait to have another girl around who could teach me how to put on makeup and other things teenage girls did. I imagined us doing one another's hair and things like that. When she walked through the door, I was taken back by how beautiful she was. I must have felt like an annoying puppy to her because I just followed her around.

"Ginny really struggled being a part of a regular family for a long time. She argued with my mom and dad about curfew rules and one day after school, she started yelling at me for using her makeup. We'd fought before that, but I'd never seen her get that angry. Her face was red as she walked toward me with the knife she was using to cut a sandwich she'd made for herself. I panicked and ran into the bathroom. I heard the knife hit the bathroom door. She begged me not to tell my dad and I didn't because I didn't want to make her more angry.

"That same night, she came into my room and said, 'Susan, I'm sorry I got mad earlier. I didn't mean to hurt you.'"

I paused again and turned to look at Matt. I could tell he was still confused about what this had to do with Mom's drinking, but he was patiently following my story.

"As time went on, our relationship grew stronger and she loved having me around. One time, she took me to a carnival to meet a guy she was talking to. As soon as we got there, she pulled out a pack of cigarettes and handed me one, telling me to try it. I told her I didn't smoke, but she called me a wimp and said it was no big deal. Of course, when I took a puff, I started to cough. She just laughed and walked away with the boy she'd just met. I watched the two of them, but he made me uncomfortable.

"She had a cup with some red punch in it, and she handed it to me, telling me to take a drink. I grabbed the cup and took a big sip. It smelled funny. They both began to laugh. 'See. Now you're cool,' she said.

"When I got home that night, I went straight to my room because I smelled bad from the punch I'd been drinking with alcohol in it. I felt sick, but I didn't want her to think I wasn't as cool as she was, so I just lay there in my bed and cried."

I explained to Matt that as time went on, her behavior really started to become defiant until one day, she ran away. She'd been gone for some time when she finally called my mom. She was living in northern California with a man and said they were engaged. She wanted to come see us around Mother's Day.

I was thirteen when my mom received the call from the Berkley Police Department that Ginny had been murdered. We were all in a tailspin the minute we received the news. My dad tried to help with the investigation into her death, but there were no leads. We were all devastated. My mom and dad flew up to the Bay Area for the viewing and burial. Ryan had been born not long after Ginny ran away, and I stayed in California with him at a neighbor's house.

I'd been angry with my parents for not allowing me to join them for the funeral. I wanted to say good-bye too. I felt hollow knowing that I would never see her again. When my parents came home, it took me a couple of days to talk to them about it.

"My mom started drinking more after work, and that worried me," I admitted. "She had multiple drinks every day after work, and her demeanor changed, like she was angry. I didn't know what to do about it, so I finally talked to my dad and told him that she scared me when she was drinking a lot. It upset him when I told him about the fights she and I had when she'd been drinking.

"It all came to a head one night, and my mom and dad got into a yelling match in the kitchen. Then I heard her scream something at him, slam the front door, and drive off. I came into the living room and found my dad sitting on the couch with tears in his eyes. He looked so defeated. He saw me standing there and apologized for the fight. He asked if Ryan heard them fighting. I told him Ryan was still asleep and probably hadn't heard anything just to make him feel better. I asked him where my mom had gone, and he said he didn't know. That night was the first time I heard my dad's true commitment to the marriage. He said he'd grown up with alcoholic parents and wasn't going to let my mom's drinking ruin their lives together. He would do whatever it took to help her because he loved her.

"I went back to my room, and minutes later, I heard my mom come home. There was crying and then it went quiet. The next morning, I asked my dad if everything was okay and he said that my mom had promised to stop drinking. She'd been sad about Ginny and thought drinking would make her feel better."

As I lay in bed remembering what had happened when Ginny died, I thought about my dad telling me that when people go through sad times, they sometimes use things like alcohol to numb their pain. That's what my mom was doing.

6

Depression

Watching my mom handling the loss of my dad the same way she did with Ginny's death was hard. I felt guilty that I couldn't do anything to help her pain or my brother's pain because I was struggling with my own emotions.

My mom and I both were struggling to handle our emotions, and when she drank, her anger rose. I was at a loss about how to handle it because I was just a kid and my own pain was deep and dark. I had fantasies about dying daily. I tried to find some joy, but there was none to be found. I didn't sleep because my brain wouldn't shut off, especially at night. Every time I allowed my eyes to shut, the vision of my dad's body slumped against his truck crept into my mind and any possibility of sleep evaporated.

A week after my dad's funeral, Mom said that the LAPD victim advocate wanted to get us all into therapy. I had never been seen by a therapist before, and I was kind of interested to see if one would be able to free my mind from the dark thoughts. I was desperate for an adult to help me navigate all of the thoughts that permeated my brain every day and all the emotions I was trying to manage. I felt lost in it all.

Appointments with a therapist were scheduled for my mom and me, and as I walked into the therapist's office, I felt empty and nauseous. It had taken everything in me just to shower and get ready for the appointment. I sat down on the chair next to my mom with my game face on. Mom had no idea what was happening inside me.

My name was called and I followed a woman into a tiny office that had apparently been designed for children. There were tiny tables with pads of paper and pens, and stuffed animals and toys were lined up by the wall next to the door. I grabbed a well-loved teddy bear that was stuffed into a basket and held it tight.

The therapist came in and introduced himself. He was an older man with white hair and round-rimmed glasses that barely stayed up on the bridge of his nose. He sat down across from me and said, "Hi, Susan. This session is only a get to know one another conversation."

"I thought you were supposed to ask me a bunch of questions," I replied. I felt a lump start to form in my throat.

"Let me tell you that you are in a safe space to talk about your feelings," he said.

A little part of me hoped I didn't have to stay too long so that I didn't say the wrong things to him. I talked to him about my family background, my boyfriend, and feeling alone. He called it a grief journey. I didn't have my own word so I just took his.

Whatever it was called, I felt alone. My mom was too consumed by her sadness and my brother's sadness to notice I was struggling. I told him about feeling like I was on an island alone. That led to enough of a conversation that I just stuffed the dark feelings back down. I never brought up the fact that I was swimming in many feelings I didn't understand. I guess I was afraid of asking about them.

He didn't ask questions, so I just went with the feelings of abandonment I felt were important to dive into. I never alluded to the image I kept having of drowning in deep water and looking up to see the sunlight bounce off the water above, as if I were so blinded by the brightness that I couldn't come up for air. I kept waiting for my mom to throw me a life raft, but it never came. That represented *my* pain, and I had no sense of what it was like for her to lose the love of her life. All I knew was that my dad had always been the one to throw me a life raft when I needed one, and now that help was gone.

Emotional abandonment was the word the therapist used to describe my experience with my mom. I was a teen who needed the reassurance from my mom that we would be okay, and it wasn't forthcoming.

During another session, we talked about my anger toward the people responsible for my dad's death and toward God for allowing that horrific thing to happen to my family. I felt that God had also abandoned me. Rage built up in me and my throat became dry as I talked. I had water next to me and took a sip just as the timer went off. I left feeling even more frustrated than I had been when I arrived for the session. He hadn't even given me ideas about how to approach my mom. I wasn't impressed with my therapist or the therapy.

A couple of weeks into therapy, my mom told me that one of the nuns from our church was going to take me to lunch the next day. Given how I was feeling about God at that moment, I wasn't too crazy about spending time with a nun. I dragged myself out of bed the next morning and managed to get dressed. I hadn't been sleeping well, and I was feeling a little foggy. I ran a brush through my hair and went into the living room to wait for this woman of God to take me to lunch.

When the doorbell rang and I answered it, a lady wearing street clothes stood at the door with a smile on her face. "You must be Susan," she said. I'd thought nuns always wore their habits, but this one was wasn't. She stepped into our entry way to shake my hand.

Mom came around the corner to greet us and thank the nun for taking me to lunch. I put on my fake happy face and followed the nun to her car. On our way to the restaurant, she was pretty quiet, which was fine with me. I could feel my nervousness rising. By the time we arrived at the restaurant, my palms were sweating and my stomach felt a little queasy, so I excused myself and went to the restroom to splash a little cold water on my face. When I met her at the table, she had a smile on her face, and it wasn't long before she started to talk to me about grief and death. The more she talked to me, the more knotted my stomach felt.

"I know how much your father's death has hurt you," she said. "But you need to find it in your heart to forgive the men responsible for his death."

I was furious. "Take me home," I replied. "I'm done with this lunch."

We left, and as soon as we pulled into the driveway at my house, I jumped out of the car and went inside. My mom was sitting on the couch in the living room watching TV, and before she could ask me how the lunch went, I snapped at her. "Don't ever do that to me again!" Then I retreated to my room for the rest of the afternoon.

I kept thinking about my next therapy session and decided that this situation was definitely going to be a topic for discussion. When I went to my session a couple of days later, I was still angry with my mom for setting me up with the nun. She hadn't even apologized, and I was hurt.

Though I had a lump in my throat, I described the lunch date with the nun and said I felt my mom had been trying to use the nun to fix me. It was the first time I'd been that expressive about my emotions.

As tears streamed down my face and my hand clenched onto my tear soaked tissue, he said, "Susan, you need to give your mother a break. I'm sure she was just trying to do something nice for you."

His tone left me feeling defeated. The bell on his timer went off and once again I left feeling worse.

After almost a year of seeing the therapist, he told me that all of the emotions I'd been dealing with were normal and I was handling them just fine, so he wouldn't have to see me anymore. He even called me a well-rounded young lady.

The well-rounded young lady that he saw handling things just fine was still struggling every day. I'd never told him about all the darkness I felt. Every time I got close, something told me to shelf it.

Two weeks after my therapy journey ended, I started to cry deep sobs in the shower. As the water slid down my face, every muscle and bone in my body seemed to ache. I could barely hold my head up as the water collected under my feet. My stomach felt empty and nauseous, and it was as if I were in a deep, dark cavern. I'd never felt that way before—not even when Ginny died. I didn't even have the energy to reach over to shut the water off and reach out into the steamy bathroom to grab the half-crumpled towel laying across the toilet seat.

Every day, I longed to hear my dad's voice. Some days those thoughts would consume me. I would go through my day physically but my head was in the clouds. These were some of the thoughts and emotions I'd never talked to my therapist about. I just kept my brave face on and talked about whatever he wanted to talk about. He never asked about my sadness.

My boyfriend Matt was the only one who knew my pain. But even he didn't know all of it. I didn't tell him that I'd thought about taking a bunch of pills to end my life so I could be with my dad again. Thoughts like that caused aching pain that felt like someone was ripping my heart out through my stomach. Those thoughts would often leave as fast as they came, and I felt guilty about having them. But I didn't want anyone to know about them, not even a therapist.

Part of the guilt I felt stemmed from the trauma Ryan had suffered the night my dad was killed. I kept telling myself that his pain was greater than mine. He'd huddled down in my dad's truck when my dad told him to duck. And as the bullets hit the truck, he had no idea what was happening. After it was over, he opened the door and ran around to the other side and held my dad, not knowing he was gone. He'd witnessed that horrific scene, not me. I'd seen the aftermath, but he'd been there when it happened. I felt guilty, even though I hadn't been there when it happened and couldn't have done anything to stop it if I *had* been there. And I didn't know how to help him.

My relationship with my mom was fractured and I didn't know how to fix it either.

I'd been putting on a strong front and that façade had apparently fooled everyone into thinking I was stronger than I really was. I never told anyone that when I closed my eyes at night, I saw my dad's body draped in the white cloth and him slumped half against his truck. It was like having a horrible movie scene played over and over in my head. The only things that made my mind right were my memories of him during better and funnier times in my life.

7

Memories and Milestones

One memory hit me as I sat at a local beauty school waiting to get my hair done for my senior prom. As the smell of perm solutions and acrylic polish permeated my nose, the memory of the last time I was there came flooding in.

It was the summer before my junior year. I begged my parents to let me get highlights in my hair. I would pay for it myself with my babysitting money. I couldn't afford a regular salon, so I made an appointment at the local beauty school. All the way to my appointment, my dad kept saying, "Honey, you're beautiful just the way you are. You don't need highlights."

I was fifteen years old and in modeling school. All the girls had highlights.

I couldn't contain my excitement when he dropped me off at the beauty school. I had a wrinkled up magazine page that had the perfect picture of what I wanted my hair to look like. I'd been a brunette my whole life and the thought of the new look made me smile. I kept thinking that once my mom and dad saw my new hair, they would love it. It wasn't a lot of highlights, so it wouldn't be too drastic.

I showed the student the photo and she applied highlighter to my hair. But as she started to remove what seemed like a million foils from my head at the shampoo bowl, the look on her face told me something wasn't right. I played out scenarios in my head of how angry my parents would be if my hair was more extreme than I'd intended it to be. The student stylist carefully washed and conditioned my locks with the thickest stuff I had ever seen.

As we made our way back to her chair, I saw all the eyes around us zero in on my head. When she picked up the blow dryer and started to dry my hair, I looked in the mirror and gasped. I was a total blonde! As she dried my hair, I prayed that somehow it would be darker by the time my dad came to pick me up. She finished and I asked if I could use a phone. Nervously, I called my house and dad answered. I told him I was done and he said he'd be there soon to pick me up.

As I sat in the front of the beauty school, I started to freak out. I watched the cars whiz by on the busy street and finally caught a glimpse of my dad's truck coming toward me. But instead of stopping, he drove on by. A couple of minutes later, he came around again, looked right at me, and drove past me again. On his third pass, I waved my hands in the air as he approached, and this time, he realized that the blonde girl was me.

He said nothing when I got into the truck, but every once in a while, he would look over at me, shake his head, and smile. When we got home, I could tell that the suspense of the story was killing him. He shut the truck off, looked at me, and said, "Was that what you wanted? Don't worry, honey. It will grow out."

We both laughed.

"No, that isn't what I wanted, but I think the girl put too much bleach in my hair," I said.

The memory of that experience with him made me smile, but as I came back to the present moment, I realized that he wouldn't be there to see my prom hair and tell me it looked pretty. There were many people at the beauty school that day, and I could feel the eyes of some of them on me as they realized I was the girl whose dad had been killed. There was quiet whispering, and a couple of the ladies came over to me and said "We're so sorry about your dad. We hope your mom and little brother are doing okay."

It felt strange to be recognized in that way. I was a girl getting her hair styled for prom. I should be excited about it. But as the women continued to talk to me, I stopped hearing them. I felt sad and disassociated from what was happening around me.

I was so anxious that I sprang from the chair before the student could do my final spray. I looked into the mirror and saw that my eyes were starting to well up with tears. I left before the tears could melt my makeup. As I drove home and away from that place, I began to feel peaceful again. Even happy. It was as if a switch had turned on inside my body.

I arrived home and excitement filled me as I got into my beautiful white dress. Matt would be there soon, and I couldn't wait to see how handsome he would look in his white tux.

My mom and I chose the limo together—a sleek, dark red-and-black 1938 Bentley. Everyone else wanted a stretch limo, but I wanted to be different.

Matt pulled up in his own car, and when he stepped out of it, my eyes were filled with the vision of him in his white tux with tails, shiny white patent leather shoes, and his perfectly styled flattop haircut. I felt so much pride in my heart that he was mine.

The Bentley appeared around the corner and pulled into the driveway. It was more beautiful than the picture of it had been. The neighbors all came out to see it and watch my mom take a million photos. So many pictures were being snapped, Matt and I felt like we had our own paparazzi.

It was time to pick up the couple riding with us and make some fun memories, but I still felt that emptiness of missing my dad. I wondered if he was watching me and if he liked my dress.

We arrived at the pre-prom party late, and everyone was leaving. The Bentley chose that moment to break down. She needed a new battery. As we waited for the new battery to arrive, Matt checked out the backyard at the site where the pre-prom party had been and discovered a champagne fountain with melted sherbet still floating on top. He decided to fill an empty bottle and bring it to the car. We weren't going anywhere for a while and decided to enjoy it.

Once the new battery arrived and was installed, we were off to prom. We had fun, but all the sugar from the champagne gave Matt a headache. It made me smile to think that the whole story of the broken down Bentley and the leftover champagne would have cracked up my dad.

During my last days of high school, we were invited to the National Police Week ceremony at the National Law Enforcement Officers Memorial. I would be able to bring Matt with us, and knowing he would be there with me made me feel better. I didn't know what to expect.

As we stepped off of the plane, the air felt thick and humid. The excitement I had felt earlier had turned to anxiousness. There was so much talk about logistics with the coordinators that it brought me back to the day of the funeral again. As we arrived at the hotel, I looked around and saw people who seemed like police family, but no one really talked to much. I recognized the blank stares I saw in others because they mirrored my own. People were milling about with blue ribbons on their jackets and shirts. My mom knew some of the representatives, so that was helpful to us.

The morning of the ceremony, we went by shuttle buses to Judiciary Square where the event was to be held. I looked around in the bus and wondered what happened to the families of other officers who were being honored. As we approached Judiciary Square, I grabbed Matt's hand and he gave me smile. With Matt at my side, I knew I could get through whatever the day would bring.

Many uniformed officers were stationed around the square, and we were escorted into the park by representatives of California and Los Angeles. There were hundreds of people everywhere I looked. I realized that we had joined a club no one wants to join. As we stepped out of our bus, I saw others streaming from other buses that had carried families, and I no longer felt alone.

An overwhelming wave of emotion swept over me when we approached the wall with the names of the fallen. My dad's name would forever be etched in that wall, and I felt both pride and grief: I was proud that he was honored in that way but felt grief because he was there because he was one of fallen officers. My eyes filled with tears as we were led to the seats that had been reserved for us. Memories of the funeral came crashing over me like a wave. When we sat down, Matt took my hand again. It was a lot to take in.

Every family like us sat in anticipation of the honor guard and of "Amazing Grace" being played by the bagpipers—just as these activities had been performed at every funeral of the brave men and women of law enforcement. I knew that I would not be the only person who would feel every muscle tense up the minute the first sound came from the bagpipes.

The name of every officer who had fallen that year was read. Then we stood up for a moment of silence for the fallen and listened to the politicians vow to do a better job of protecting law enforcement. After the ceremony, we were lead to the computer by the wall to see where we could see my dad's name and make a pencil rubbing to take back with us. As I watched

Matt make the rubbing, the now familiar feeling of dreamlike thoughts came over me again. Was I going backwards in healing or was this part of the healing?

Not long after the ceremony in Washington, D.C., I experienced another pinnacle event: my graduation. Every time I thought about it, I felt empty. As a little girl, I'd dreamed of the day both my parents would watch me graduate high school. Now I knew that fantasy would never become reality. I was stressed out in the months leading to my graduation day and spent every day after my father's death in a fog. I slipped in and out of my classes continuously because my attention span was very short. I struggled to stay on top of my grades and navigate normal high school activities.

Graduation day was hot that June, and as we were led onto the field, sweat beaded underneath my white graduation gown. As thoughts of my dad swirled into my head, I looked up in the stands to see my family. There were LAPD officers present, along with family friends. Matt wasn't there because his sister was graduating at another high school at the same time, and I felt his absence.

LAPD officers were standing at attention on the sidelines of the field. I was blown away. Not only did it make me feel special, but I also felt they had my back. I could see my mom trying to wave at me as I sat waiting for the ceremony to start, and it felt good to see her excitement for me.

When they called my name, I stepped up to the stage and accepted my diploma. I knew my life would change again, and

I didn't know how I was going to navigate my grief without my friends every day.

8

On My Own

I went right back to school a month after graduation. The Fashion Institute of Design and Merchandising was calling my name and I answered. After graduation, Mom found out that there were scholarships available for the children of fallen LAPD officers, so I applied for and got one.

I believed that if I stayed really busy, I wouldn't have time to dwell on my loss and sadness.

I continued to present a happy face, and no one at my school knew who I was or what had happened. I felt safe from questions and explanations. I was done talking about it. I just craved some sense of normalcy in my life and felt I could have my old life back if I just pretended well enough. Unfortunately, denial doesn't work that way. The feelings of loneliness, anger, and sadness did not end. I was not in a good enough place mentally to be in school and dropped out after eight months.

My relationship with my mom became even more tense. I couldn't even communicate with her because I believed nothing

I might say would be the right thing and it would lead to a fight. It felt hopeless. Everything in my life was in turmoil, and I wasn't sure if our relationship would survive. I didn't know what to do to help her. Dad always knew just the right thing to say to navigate through the stress of her anger. He was the mediator, the calm voice that kept me centered. I was really having a hard time without his wise words and caring manor. I was still a kid who needed my mother to be present, but she was caught up in her grief. I hoped things between us would calm down over time, and I sat on the sidelines waiting for the day that would happen.

I had so many stressors that there were times I thought my head would explode. I had a lot to look forward to, but sadness was still a factor in my everyday life. Walking on eggshells and people pleasing became my modus operandi and I avoided telling my mom anything about how I felt because I didn't want to make things harder for her.

I found myself hiding from the true me with a phony mask of "I'm fine" stretched across my face as I continued to witness my mom's self-destructive drinking habits. Every day, I tried my hardest to be what she needed, and every day, I felt I failed her. It felt as if I'd lost her too the day my dad was taken from us.

I needed to get out of the house. I had been doing some research on apartments with one of my friends and decided it was time to move out on my own. I hoped we could heal our relationship if we no longer lived under the same roof. I was ready to leave the nest, and I decided my eighteenth birthday in October would be a good time to do it.

My stomach was in knots on my birthday and guilt began to form in my brain as I prepared to approach my mom about moving out. But I realized I had to do it for the sake of all three of us. As soon as I entered the house, my mother came toward me from the kitchen looking angry. Immediately, I started to retreat towards my room. That didn't deter her.

"Where have you been?" she screamed. "The kitchen hasn't been cleaned and you're out doing whatever!"

When Ryan popped his head out of his room, mom shoved him back in and held the door closed. I could smell the slight hint of rum coming from the cup in her other hand.

I feel like running, but my anger was telling me I'd had enough. "I'm moving out!" I replied. "I can't live here anymore with you constantly yelling at me!"

With every word coming from my mouth, she became more frustrated. "You aren't going anywhere until the first of next year!" she said, red-faced.

I stayed and searched for my first apartment. I made a new friend who was also planning to move out on her own, and we found a two bedroom apartment that would be ready in January. The day of the move, I was sad to leave Ryan, guilty to be moving out, and excited for my first journey on my own.

My roommate and I decided to live together for a year: a year of finding my own peace; a year of healing and not feeling the anxiousness of walking on eggshells at home. I wasn't trying to make my mom out to be a monster. I'd just been living with a parent who found it hard to be present and responsive to my emotional needs. I knew she was trying to deal with her own grief and sadness every day. I also knew she had to deal with my eight-year-old brother and the pain he was feeling about losing his dad. I needed to break away to find my own place of healing, and I wanted to feel something other than resentment.

Living on my own made me feel free, but it wasn't as easy as I thought it would be. Matt's parents were transferred to Minnesota and he decided to stay in California. He was living in a converted garage at the home of a good friend's parents. Being almost a thousand miles away from his parents and sisters was hard for both of us. They had been a second family to me.

A couple of days after they moved, Matt and I decided to go to his old house and park across the street. As we stared at his childhood home, Matt's eyes filled with tears. Even though they were only in another state, I could feel the pain of not having them close enough to see. I started to weep too, and we cried together as we listened to the U2 song, "Red Hill Town," playing on the radio. When the song was finished, we dried our tears and left.

Eight months into living with my roommate, I was struggling with our living arrangement. My roommate and I were frustrating each other and thinking that after our lease was up, we would part ways.

In the months after I moved out, my mom and I occasionally had lunch together. We were in a place in our relationship where we could talk about things that mattered, so during one of our lunches, I told her about my frustration with my room-mate. She listened to me as I explained that I wanted to stay on my own but not with her after the lease was up.

"Why don't you and Matt get a place together?" she suggested. She must have seen the look of shock on my face as those words came out of her mouth because she added, "I would feel better with you living with him. You'd be safer."

My mom was giving mom advice, which was something I'd wanted for a long time, and it made me happy. I couldn't wait to talk to Matt. She was right: Matt was my safe place. And I thought we could make it work. I called Matt as soon as I got home and we made plans for him to come over that night because my roommate would be out that evening.

"I told her about what is happening here with my roommate."

"What did she say about it?"

"She said that maybe you and I should move in together."

I could tell from the utter shock on his face that he didn't believe me.

"How did your lunch go with your mom?" he asked when he arrived. me. I laughed. "What do you think about that plan?"

He grabbed me, hugged me, and said he thought it was a great idea.

Finding the right apartment took some time, but we found the perfect little place in Van Nuys just in time for my lease to end with my roommate. Our one bedroom, one bath apartment was on the interior of the building, facing the pool. We had fun creating our home together. I adorned it in pretty shades of coral with seafoam green couches. Nagel posters in cheap black frames lined the walls.

That move represented a giant step in our relationship.

9

The Trials

Not long after we moved into our apartment, the trials started for the men involved in my dad's murder. We were told by the district attorney that there would be two separate trials because there were five defendants. The trials would take place at the courthouse very close to my apartment. That sent me into anxiety every day. I awoke with a dry mouth and skin that felt like it was coming off my body. I would have to relive that night, and this time, there will be details that I had sheltered my younger self from knowing.

I sat in my car in silence waiting a while before turning the key, starting my car, and heading out with the bustling news coverage of the trial. I wanted to pretend it wasn't happening, but there was no way to avoid it. Five men had conspired and executed the first man I'd ever loved: my daddy. Now they were being tried and the trial was making headlines.

I read some self-help books, hoping to self-heal, but they weren't enough help for me to sustain the enormous amount of pain headed toward me like a freight train. I would wake in the morning to the news coverage of the previous day's court proceedings. It all came flooding back as I watched the news story images of my dad's truck with him next to it, covered by a white sheet. Being constantly reminded of the horrific details felt like gut punches.

I chose to refrain from attending the trial hearings with my mom. She had friends with her for support. I stayed in my space to work through my feelings as best I could. The news reports of the trials were in the newspaper every morning with all of the graphic details in black-and-white.

A couple of weeks into the July 1988 trial, my mom called to warn me that there were details coming out of the testimony from several witnesses that the defendant I'll call Lago not only wanted my dad dead but also wouldn't mind if his whole family died. Especially Ryan, because Lago believed he would grow up to be a cop like his dad, according to the testimony from one witness. I felt a lump in my throat as she told me he'd planned the killing for months. Photographs had been entered into evidence that showed the front of my childhood home, and some even included Matt's blue Volkswagen Karmann Ghia parked in front. That meant that we were all in danger at that time.

"He didn't care who died as long as my dad was killed," she said.

Mom wanted to keep me informed, but sometimes what she told me was just too much to swallow. On the one hand, those conversations didn't feel healthy, but on the other, I had to admit that I'd been angry when my parents had hidden certain details about Ginny's death. *Should* I know every detail? Some days I felt she didn't know when to limit the information.

Three weeks into the trial, and one of the defendants testified that he'd put glue into the chamber of the MAC-10 that was used in the first attempt to kill my father. The gun had jammed, rendering it unable to fire. If he hadn't wanted Lago to be successful, I wondered why hadn't he told the police department the plan instead of trying to thwart the execution by compromising the gun.

Another defendant turned state's evidence, so there was a chance he would not get convicted. I didn't understand all the terms my mom threw at me on our calls, but I understood enough to know that two of the defendants might not be convicted.

As the trial continued, I looked up legal terms I didn't know in an attempt to understand them. And as information continued to come out during the trial, I felt afraid to tell Matt that he had possibly been in danger too. I had no idea that he'd been reading the newspapers with all of the details of the trial testimony.

My body and mind felt heavy, and it was a struggle to get out of bed to go to work. I was working as an assistant secretary for a tile company, and I'd always had a great attitude at work. But I was submerged in the media frenzy that followed the trial and was dealing with anger and frustration that were difficult to shut down. I headed to work one morning, started up the car, and put on my favorite music station hoping for a little peace before I had to face my day. Instead, I heard a breaking news story about what happened during the trial the previous day. Anxiousness rose from my feet to my head.

As I came in through the warehouse door at work, I was met by my coworkers. I usually joked with them as I made my way through the warehouse to my office, but that day, I wasn't feeling it. One of my coworkers saw the scowl on my face and tossed a box at me to get me to laugh. That didn't happen. Instead, I became frustrated and snapped at him. He was a nice guy, but he was on the receiving end of my frustration that day.

My boss was waiting for me at my desk and told me to put my purse down and follow him. We went down the hall, and I saw the coworker I'd snapped at standing in front of an empty office. "Whatever is going on between you two, you're going into this office to privately hash it out," my boss said. "And you can't come out until the issue is resolved."

I didn't have an issue with him, so I was perplexed. We went into the office, shut the door, and sat down. He looked nervous. I had never seen him like this, so I was concerned.

"I know why you snapped at me," he said. "I've been following your dad's trial and I know that all the men involved are black. You snapped at me because I'm a black man too."

"Why do you think that would matter?" I replied.

"The man who killed your father is black, and I wouldn't blame you if you hated black men."

"You didn't kill my father. It doesn't matter that *they're* black. They're five individuals who planned the killing of another human being."

He looked at me with astonishment.

"I'm sorry I took my frustration out on you earlier," I said. "I woke up wanting to get away from the coverage of the trial but heard it on the radio this morning. I apologize."

He apologized too and we hugged. I left that room feeling I had just learned a lesson about how people perceived me based on their own feelings of how *they* would feel. I felt sad as I headed back to my supervisor's office to let him know everything was fine.

That night I received a call from my mom, the youngest defendant—a man I'll call Vic—had begun his testimony, and it had been extremely hard for my mom to hear. She'd seen the MAC-10 used in the killing, and witnesses had testified that he was an integral part of the planning with Lago. He'd been told by Lago that he needed to get rid of the main witness in his upcoming trial, and Lago had said that witness was a security guard. Lago wanted Vic to find someone to take out the security guard. Lago told him to follow the person they were going to kill to discover his daily routines so the hit could happen when he was most vulnerable. Vic wanted to make a name for himself with Lago so he could have what Lago had: the flash of cash, the cars, and the women.

Vic found a man for the hit, offered him ten thousand dollars to do it, and said it needed to happen the next day. He and Lago would supply the gun, gloves, and car needed for the hit. Vic and the man doing the hit followed the supposed security guard to his son's school, but the hit man backed out when he saw that a child could be killed. Upset and frustrated, Vic returned to Lago to let him know what happened, and according to witness testimony, Lago passed the gun to Vic to handle the job himself. Vic wanted to impress Lago and accepted the job. He left to do more surveillance. But this plan failed too because Vic couldn't move forward with the hit. Lago became angered with the incompetency of his crew.

My mom told me she'd heard in testimony that Lago hated my dad and decided to do the hit himself but recruited more help to get the job done. I couldn't hear any more details and ended the call. Matt was still at work, so I sat on the couch and sobbed by myself. Being alone with my thoughts was not a good place to be. I couldn't wrap my head around everything I was hearing: Lago having such hatred for my dad and elaborate planning that went on for months. I felt helpless and my world felt violated.

Each day during the nine months of the trials, my head was filled with the gory details of my dad's demise and the lengths Lago and his crew went to in making it happen.

Many parts of the puzzle started to come together for me. When I was still in high school in 1986, Lago was dating a girl I was in drill team with. Allegedly, he tried to get her to befriend me in hopes that I would bring her to my house and she could report back the layout of the house and any other intel about my family. Details like that one oozed from the testimony, and I went to bed each night with information that sent shivers down my spine and made me sick to my stomach.

One day my mom called and blurted out, "Susan, he got married today in the middle of the trial."

"Who got married?" I asked.

"Lago got married. We broke for lunch and all of a sudden, in walked this girl who works for his attorney. She was dressed in white, and she had her bridesmaids walking behind her. Another judge appeared and they got married."

I couldn't believe my ears.

"I can't make up this shit!" Mom added.

"I'm so sorry you had to see that circus!" I replied.

Circus was the right word to use when it came to the trials. I couldn't wait for them to end.

Finally, in July 1988, Lago and his main accomplice, a man I'll call Rudy who drove the vehicle used in the assassination, were found guilty. Lago was convicted on three counts: first degree murder with special circumstances (killing a police officer); conspiracy to commit murder; and attempted murder (the original case my dad was on, the attempted murder of the theater manager).

In August 1988, Rudy was convicted of first degree murder with special circumstances and conspiracy to commit murder. He was sentenced to life without the possibility of parole. Vic was convicted of conspiracy to commit murder because of his participation in planning the killing. The other two defendants were acquitted.

We were told that at the sentencing, the victims would be able to make a statement. I woke up the day the sentencing was to take place with a feeling of dread, in large measure because I knew I would face Lago, look into his eyes, and pour out my sadness. I also thought that moment would not belong to me alone because the courtroom would be filled with his family and the media. Anxiety pierced my body as I stood at my bathroom mirror trying to keep it together enough to get my hair and makeup finished.

As I waited for my mom to pick me up, I kept going through the statement I'd prepared, which I'd written down and would give voice to at the sentencing—a voice that had felt stifled for three years. When Mom pulled up to the curb and I got in, she said, "Are you ready for this? I'm not sure where we're supposed to go, so I'll talk to the district attorney when we get there."

I think both of us were struggling with how we were going to get through that day. I was stuffing down the many emotions I was feeling in an attempt to contain them until I needed them at the podium in court. I needed to be brave to show Lago and everyone else that I was strong and that I was my father's daughter.

We arrived and found the district attorney. He escorted us into the courtroom and to the seats behind the attorneys. I could feel the hard stares and heard the sneers and comments coming from Lago's family there for his support. They had no idea how much pain their family member had put on my family.

From the corner of my eye, I saw Lago being escorted into the courtroom. Chills ran up my spine as I stared at him sitting in the seat next to his attorney. His face was blank with no expression. Then he actually laughed with his attorney. I kept wondering how a person could laugh at such a time.

The judge entered and the room grew silent. Lago's attorney stood up, asked that the verdict be vacated, and requested a new trial. He reminded me of a rat with his unruly hair, pointed nose, and small beady eyes behind his bifocal glasses. The judge saw through his manipulation and denied his request.

I sat with my crumpled statement in my sweaty palms, waiting for the judge to call my name. "Go ahead, and don't worry about everyone else in this courtroom," she said when it was my turn to make a statement.

My eyes were filled with tears and my knees began to buckle as I made my way to the podium. I put my paper down in front of me. Lago turned to me and I looked right at him. The darkness in his eyes and his cold stare scared me to my core. But instead of retreating, I fought my fear and proceeded to speak.

"Your Honor, my name is Susan Williams. I'm the daughter of Detective Tom Williams. For the past three years, my life has been a nightmare, one that started on October 31, 1985. My life was shattered when my dad was killed. He was a loving, caring, and respected man. He fought for what he believed in. I don't know why a man so loving could die the way he did. He certainly didn't deserve the death sentence that was put upon him. But this I know: Lago and Rudy deserve everything that is coming to them.

"Their sentences will never bring my father back to us, but at least I know they will suffer not being with their families. It is nearly Christmas, which makes it extremely hard because Christmas is for family. My family has been shattered and my dad won't be home for Christmas. He won't be there for all the important things in my life." Once I finished, I caught Lago's gaze. No remorse filled his expression.

My mom then stood up and spoke her truth, her pain, and her anger. I could hear the sniffles of the people behind me and saw the tears in the eyes of our friends in court.

When my mom finished, Lago's attorney addressed the judge to let her know that Lago had something to say. Lago stood up and puffed his chest. He demanded better treatment in prison. He spoke of the Bible and said the judge should not sentence him to death because she would be answering to God if she did. I sat there in disbelief as he pontificated on how the case against him had been set up by LAPD. Absolutely no remorseful words came out of his mouth. I was stunned, and I saw my mom's posture tighten.

The judge interrupted him and said it was time for his sentencing. Attorneys for both the prosecution and defense spoke as we sat impatiently waiting to hear the sentence. Finally, the judge spoke. "You are hereby sentenced to death by lethal injection for the first degree murder of Detective Thomas C. Williams."

The courtroom erupted. His family wept and yelled for him as he was quickly taken away. A cat and mouse chase ensued as reporters attempted to catch us as we headed toward the back of the building. Cameras were in my face as I tried to escape.

"How do you feel about the sentence?" one blurted out.

"Do you feel closure?" another asked.

Questions were flung at us from every direction, but we finally escaped out the back door. As we made our way to the parking garage, I recognized a woman behind me as one of the people who had been there for Lago. I heard comments being made about how we must have loved that LAPD had done what they could to hang it on Lago.

Anger and sadness filled my soul that day. I wasn't sure how I was supposed to feel, but closure and happiness was not what I felt.

10

Engagement and Wedding

The year after the trials ended, life seemed to be getting better. I was about to turn twenty-one, I was attending a beauty school to get my career going, and Matt and I were building a home together in Palmdale, California. Matt's youngest sister was now in California and living with my mom temporarily. Things seemed to be going in the right direction.

Except for my hair that is.

At beauty school, we often used ourselves as guinea pigs. Unfortunately, I was the recipient of bad color, bad haircuts, and the doozy of them all, a bad perm. I thought a perm would cover up all the other mistakes. Instead I ended up looking like the cartoon character Judy Jetson. My bob haircut and perm made me look like a frizzy poodle.

For my birthday that year, Matt decided to throw me a party at our friend's house in the valley. There I was with my Judy Jetson hair, large hoop earrings, MC Hammer pants, and cropped sweater.

I was excited to be able to see all of my friends. We arrived at Robert's house, we made our way to the backyard where a DJ had set up for the night. The night was beautiful and I was happy to be surrounded by all our friends. I thought it couldn't get any better, but Matt had other plans.

Back indoors, as I was talking to some friends, the DJ called my name and told me to come to the DJ booth. I felt people following behind me as I made my way back outside and over to the DJ. With a giant smile on his face, he told me to turn around. When I did, there was Matt on one knee holding a beautiful ring in his hand.

"Susan, will you take my hand in marriage?" he asked.

Matt was always a little old fashioned, and I loved that about him.

He placed the princess cut diamond ring on my finger as I said, "Yes."

Then we embraced and whispered, "I love you," to one another.

Matt's sister ran up, hugged me, and said, "Welcome to our family!"

I had a smile on my face the entire night, and we ended up spending the night at Robert's house. Lying in bed and staring at my ring, I kept thinking about my dad. I knew he would be happy to see me happy, and I wondered what he would have said to us.

In the morning, I awoke to Matt smiling at me. He leaned over and told me that he had gone to see my mom a couple of days ahead of the party and asked her permission to marry me.

I started to cry, sad that my dad had not been a part of that special moment. Then I felt even sadder as I realized my mom probably felt the same way.

I didn't waste any time planning the wedding. The first thing on the docket was the date. Matt and I talked about getting married in May. My mom had lost a half-sister to cancer, and her birthday had been May 26. That date fell on a Saturday, so it was perfect. I wanted to give Mom a day she could celebrate instead of it being a sad reminder of loss. We talked to my mom and she cried when we told her that was the date we chose and why. We would turn it from a sad day into a day of love.

Mom and I were doing well and she wanted to help plan the wedding. There were still days where I had to find my happiness. I searched all the bridal stores and nothing spoke to me, so I talked to mom about designing my own dress and the bridesmaids' dresses. I wanted something more tasteful than the gaudy dresses of that time, and I thought I could use some of the things I'd learned during the brief time I'd been at The Fashion Institute of Design and Merchandising. I sketched out what I thought my perfect wedding dress would look like: a high sweetheart neckline; big puffy shoulders made of satin; a tight mermaid bodice in lace with satin underneath it; a heart-shaped cutout on the back of the bodice, exposing my back; small buttons; and a skirt with sheer ruffles that flowed onto the floor and draped into a three-foot train. That dress would make me feel like a real princess.

I planned to have four bridesmaids, a maid of honor, and a flower girl. My bridesmaids' dresses were designed a little like my dress with a shorter length in the front and draping longer in the back. They would be made of a stiff, hunter green taffeta with puffy shoulders. I designed the dresses to have a small bow that would sit along the neckline on the front.

I was so proud of my designs, and I fantasized about how pretty my girls would look in the dresses on my wedding day. I was excited about Matt's family coming to town for the wedding. Matt's two sisters, Suzanne and Julie, were going to be bridesmaids, and I looked forward to the moment when they would see the beautiful dresses I'd designed for them.

That moment came three days before the wedding. Suzanne and Julie went straight to the dress shop for a final fitting of the dresses. I had also arranged for my maid of honor Kristin to go to the shop at the same time. Unfortunately, I got caught up with other wedding details and couldn't meet them there.

As I was about to leave my apartment, Suzanne called. "Susan, we aren't wearing this dress," she said. I asked why. "We look like bozos with these huge bows on our chest."

I wanted to cry. "I don't understand. The bow was supposed to be petite and pretty." I needed to find a solution. I couldn't have my bridesmaids looking like clowns, so I told the dressmaker to put the bows on the hip instead of on the bodice. While the bridesmaids had different figures, I knew that everyone's figures would be complemented by the bow. Disaster averted!

We were expecting a little more than three hundred people at the wedding, but one important guest would not be there: my dad. I awoke on my wedding morning to a bright, sunny day, but I was sad that my dad's best friend and Ryan would be walking me down the aisle, not my dad. That morning was filled with all of the excitement of the day, but the sadness that couldn't be ignored lingered.

I started my morning at the salon for my hair appointment. My hair had not grown out as long as I would have liked, so I had some extensions put in for the wedding. At the appointment, I tried to enjoy all of the happy moments. Then I dashed to my mom's house to finish getting ready. As I sat in my mom's living room, my brain was flooded with memories of my dad and happy times we'd shared. I so wished he was there sitting next to me. I yearned to hear his voice telling me how special it would be to walk me down the aisle to my love. Then anger crept into my head—anger that he'd been taken away and couldn't have this special time with me.

Some of the bridesmaids arrived ready to help me get dressed, but I had to excuse myself to go catch my breath and calm my anger. I sat on the bed in my old room, struggling to keep from crying because I didn't want to ruin the beautiful makeup I'd had done at the salon. After a couple of minutes, I popped up off the bed, dabbed my eyes, put on a smile, and joined the girls.

The remaining bridesmaids arrived, along with my flower girl. Everyone was waiting on me so they could get me dressed before the photographer arrived to take pre-wedding pictures.

As I approached them, I looked into their eyes. They knew the day was hard for me, but instead of talking about it, they just smiled at me as if to say it would be okay and that they had my back. A couple of the girls rushed me into the bedroom to get me into my dress.

As I was dressing, I heard the front door open and the sound of Matt and his parents talking. And as I looked into the mirror and caught a glimpse of the bridesmaids in their dresses, it felt a bit like we were all in costumes preparing for a performance. I was excited to be marrying Matt and I felt love from everyone around me, but it still felt as if I was going through the motions and doing what everyone needed me to be doing. My dad's presence was the missing piece.

My mom came to tell me the photographer was there and was setting up in front of the house, and I caught a glimpse of her as I made my way to the front door. I saw the pain in her eyes about that missing piece and knew we were both feeling the weight of that on the day. She silently mouthed to me that I looked beautiful.

A couple of mishaps happened that morning. While mishaps on your wedding day is never a good thing, they did manage to distract me from the pain lurking around the corner, waiting to penetrate my thoughts and steal my joy. Outside, the photographer was talking with Matt's parents. His mom, Marcia, looked beautiful in her emerald green sequined dress, and his dad, Larry, looked great in his tux. They both looked happy. Suzanne and Julie came out and we went to stand by their parents.

The photographer motioned to Marcia to come toward him. Unfortunately, he kept referring to her as *grandma*. I was mortified. I finally went over to him, gently leaned over, and said, "Please stop calling my future mother-in-law *grandma*."

Then my mom came over to let me know that one of the limos we'd ordered was not going to make it to take Marcia and Larry to the church. They would have to drive themselves. I was embarrassed, but they were very gracious and didn't care.

After all the pre-wedding pictures were done, my brides-maids and I got into the limo waiting for us and headed to the church. With all of the chaos at my mom's house, we'd lost track of time and were running late. And now we were stuck in traffic.

At the church, we rushed to collect our flowers and Kristin found my blue garter, which I had realized I wasn't wearing. We laughed as Kristin crawled under my dress and slid my garter up my legs. I'd definitely asked the right person to be my maid of honor. At that point, I felt like I was on a conveyor belt as people handed me things and made sure my dress was just right.

Ryan and Roger, my dad's best friend, were waiting for me in the sanctuary hall when I arrived. Ryan looked nervous and handsome in his tux. Roger was a lieutenant colonel in the Marines and was wearing his dress blues, white hat, and freshly polished black shoes with his sword at his hip. He looked regal. Roger was a stoic man, but tears welled up in his eyes when he saw me in my wedding gown.

Ryan and Roger stood on either side of me with one arm under each of my arms. I could feel Ryan trembling. I was thankful for my veil, which limited my vision. It was heavy and dramatic, but it was the perfect tool to cover my face and let me hide.

As we waited for the ceremony to begin, I yearned to hear my dad's voice, and just before I took my first step, I turned to Roger for reassurance. He looked down at me, tightened his arm around mine, took my hand with his other hand, and softly whispered, "He's here with us today."

The double door opened and I dug down to find strength to walk forward, down the long aisle to my love waiting for me at the front of the church. When I began to increase my pace, Roger pulled me back a little, quietly reminding me to not rush and to enjoy the moment. Roger was right! As scared as I felt having over three hundred people staring at me, my heart was feeling joy because I was marrying my true love.

As we approached Matt, I saw tears streaming down his face and heard sniffling from people in the sanctuary. I was trembling when I grabbed his hand, and he rubbed my hand in support. Ryan had tears streaming down his face and Matt left my side for a moment to embrace him and assure him that he was doing fine.

When Matt stepped back to my side and the pastor asked who was giving me away, Roger stepped forward. "We do, and her father and mother." He pulled away my veil and gently kissed my cheek, and I swore at that moment, my dad was there with me.

Everyone could feel the sadness in the room as they watched Matt and I exchange our vows and place our rings on each other's finger. But during our first kiss as husband and wife, I felt we were moving forward. And not only were we excited for the future, I believed my father was excited for us too.

Church Photo

Wedding Photo

11

Loss Turns to Happiness

Matt and I were enjoying being newlyweds, but everyone began asking us when we were having kids. I really didn't want to have kids. I didn't know why, other than the fact that I felt I needed to be a second parent to Ryan after my dad died and it was hard having that much responsibility at such a young age. I just wanted to have fun with Matt and enjoy being married.

Six months into our marriage, I was feeling a bit off and didn't know why. A friend told me I should take a pregnancy test, and all the way to the store to buy one, I was terrified. I wasn't ready to be a mom. I was anxious as I came home with the test and paced back and forth. Finally, I took the test and saw the plus sign indicating that I was pregnant. It was real. I was pregnant. All of a sudden, a burst of happiness filled my body. It was a bit confusing because I'd had strong feelings about not having kids. But now all those feelings were fading and all I felt was excitement.

Matt came home from work and I sat him down. "I know we talked about not having kids right away, but I took a test. I'm pregnant!" I blurted out.

Matt grabbed me and hugged me tight with tears in his eyes. I knew he was happy. But then we looked at each other and we both felt scared, wondering if we could do this. It didn't take long for Matt to grab the phone and call his parents, sisters, and pretty much everyone we were friends with. I wasn't sure we should say anything because I probably was only six weeks along, but we were both so happy, we just didn't care.

Three days later our elation turned to sadness when I realized that I was having a miscarriage. Anger rose up in my mind as it was happening. I was losing someone else in my life and I had no control over what my body was doing. We were devastated. After thinking I didn't want kids before I became pregnant, now all I could think of was having kids with Matt. It was incredible how many women in my life had suffered miscarriages too, and they told me that something might have been wrong with the pregnancy and my body terminated it because of that. That support gave me comfort.

Two years later, I wasn't feeling quite right again. I thought something was wrong with me, so I went to the doctor. She immediately ordered a pregnancy test. I told her I was concerned that I might have some kind of hormonal imbalance.

When the test results came back, she said, "Yes, you do have a hormonal imbalance, it will last about nine months."

"I'm pregnant?" I asked with tears in my eyes.

"Yes. It looks like you're already ten weeks pregnant," she replied.

I couldn't believe it, and I couldn't wait to race home and tell Matt. Once home, I again sat Matt down on the couch.

"How did your appointment with the doctor go?" he asked. "Are you okay?"

"I'm fine," I replied. "But she said I would probably be a little hormonal for about nine months."

He looked confused. " What?"

"We're going to have a baby."

We sat and cried together. Then I told him the doctor thought I was ten weeks pregnant and thought it would be okay to tell people if we wanted to make an announcement. Our families first. I really couldn't wait for my mom and brother to know.

I went to the store and bought a card for my mom that said, "Congratulations, Grandma." I came to her house and put it on the table by the couch in plain sight. When she came into the room, Matt and I were standing by the table.

"Mom, we have a little something for you here on the table," I said.

Mom walked over to the table to pick up the card looking confused because it wasn't her birthday or any other holiday. She opened the card and stared at it for a couple of seconds before she looked up and caught my smile. " I'm going to be a grandma?" she asked. Then she laughed. "Although grammy is better."

"Yes, mom. You're going to be a grammy!"

I felt blessed because my pregnancy was without any issues and I was the happiest I had ever been. Matt and I were excited to start our family. We didn't learn the baby's sex before he was born, so the anticipation was exciting.

After thirteen hours of labor, Trentan Thomas Snow was born on January 8, 1993. Thirteen babies were born that night, and the hospital was a little chaotic. My mom and Matt were both in the delivery room when Trentan was born, and afterward, Matt went with Trentan to the nursery while my mom went to call Matt's family with the news.

As I lay alone, sadness crept into the room. Trentan's middle name had been very deliberately chosen. He was given the name of my hero, my dad. I was sad that my father had missed the birth of his first grandchild, and I asked God to give me strength and help me to be a good mother to my beautiful baby boy.

12

The Medium and
the Movie

That same year, Mom and I were approached by a production company to do a movie about my dad's story. I had some apprehensions about the project. It made me nervous. I was right to feel that way because when I talked to the screenwriter about what transpired, it brought all the painful feelings back to the surface. That frustrated me. I had been making some progress in moving forward, and now that conversation was sending me backwards at a time when I was carrying a tiny human inside who didn't yet know this legacy. Ultimately, I agreed to move forward with the movie, in part because it *was* part of my child's legacy.

Three months after Trentan was born and during the preparation phase of the movie, Mom and I were approached again, this time by a producer for a television show based in Australia. The show featured paranormal experiences and would focus on the talents of a specific medium in Long Island, New York, named George Anderson. I had never spoke to a medium before, and I was a little scared at the prospect of meeting him but also curious about possibly being able to communicate with my dad and Ginny. I needed to know if they were at peace. The show would focus on families that had lost a loved one tragically. Even though our movie was in the works, Mom and I decided to do the show.

The production company flew me, Mom, and baby Trentan to New York. It was the first flight for my newborn son, and he was a champ, sleeping through most of it. The production company picked us up in a limousine and shuffled us off to Long Island. I became so nervous that I started to sweat. My hands tingled and I was nauseous. As mom and I were freshening up in the limo, I looked out the limo window to see that we had arrived at the medium's house. We were told he had not been given any information about our story.

We were taken into a small room where we waited to be taken to the filming room. Emotions were exploding in me, but fortunately, I had my baby to occupy my attention. I was still working through some feelings about my faith in God, and I wondered if my dad was aware of all of the wonderful things that had happened in my life, especially the birth of his grandson. In my head, I kept thinking, *Daddy do you know about your grandson? Were you in the room when I gave birth to him?* I wanted George Anderson to answer those questions during our reading.

When we were called to be filmed, I handed my baby to a lady from the production company and we were led into the filming room. A man with short blondish-gray hair approached me and held out his hand to shake mine. His smile was kind and all the feelings of nervousness left my body. I felt I had known this man my whole life, and I felt safe.

The reading started, and while the cameras, lights, and sound people in our faces were a little intimidating, I was concentrated on what Mr. Anderson was saying. He told us he felt my dad's spirit in the room with us. My dad was giving me spiritual roses in congratulations for something. Then he saw the birth of a child. "Your dad wants you to know that he was there with you," he said.

I was shocked, and my heart exploded with happiness. I hadn't even told my mom that I'd had those questions in my head earlier. Mr. Anderson went on to tell us that Ginny was also around us and that both of them were at peace. I had been filled with sadness for so long, even in the happiest of times, and now I knew both of them were around to see all the wonderful things happening in my life.

I had gone into the reading a bit skeptical, wondering if someone really could communicate with someone in spirit, but after the reading, I felt so much peace. I became a believer that day. I returned from New York with a new outlook on life after death. It was a great experience, but now we needed to get back to another reality.

Production of the movie started when Trentan was five months old. Mom and I were creative consultants on the project, which meant we would be present on set for much of the shooting. It all felt new, and I kind of felt like a celebrity. The crew were nice to us, although there were times when they looked at me as if I were a china doll that might break. It reminded me of my high school days right after Dad's murder.

One day on the set, I anxiously waited to meet the actress who was playing me, Kathleen Robertson. The director wanted us to have a private meeting so she could get to know me a little better, and I was taken to a trailer. It felt strange to be meeting the person who would be playing me, and I wondered if she would look at all like me. All I knew about her was that she came from Toronto, Canada. When she entered the trailer, I could see that she did not look like me, but she was beautiful. She had green eyes and gorgeous brown hair cut into a cute bob haircut, and I could detect her Canadian accent when she spoke. She was very sweet and very serious about her job of portraying me.

Even as surreal as it was, I really loved that perfect strangers would get a glimpse of who my dad was and a tiny glimpse into our lives. When the filming started, Trentan accompanied me and my mom on the set, bouncing around in his kangaroo sling. On occasion, Matt took a day off to come to the set with us too. The production was to take place in several areas of the San Fernando Valley. The actors included Michael Gross as my dad, Mary Kay Place as my mom, and Dean Stockwell as the lead investigator. I spoke to most of the actors on the set, and I was sure it wasn't easy for them having us there, knowing how we lost my dad.

One day on the set, I believed my dad's spirit was there. It was the scene where a jewelry store owner was robbed by Jonnie Moore's crew. (*Jonnie* was the pseudonym for Lago's character.) My dad was the key investigator in the robbery and got called to the scene. In the scene, he was walking and talking with his partner, strategizing on who could have committed the robbery. Then he pulled down on his nose gently, just like my dad did when he was deep in thought. I couldn't believe what I was witnessing.

It was as if my dad were there influencing Michael Gross to make that gesture. After the scene was finished, I approached Mr. Gross and asked him if gently pulling on his nose was something he regularly did. He looked at me in puzzlement and said no. I reminded him that I had just witnessed him do that exact thing, and when we watched the playback of that scene, he admitted he had no idea he'd done that.

I explained that my dad pulled on his nose gently when he was in deep thought, and Mr. Gross nervously laughed. Then he asked me to let him know if there were other gestures in my dad's behavior because he was honored to play him. He wanted to make sure he did my dad justice in his portrayal. Mr. Gross was a consummate professional and gracious man. That was an eye-opening lesson for me. Here was a actor who had no idea who my dad was, but he was so moved by learning about him from me that his intention was to make sure we were satisfied with his performance.

Intention was something I learned from my dad. He'd lead an intentional life, and he was always striving to be a better dad, husband, detective—a better person, in general. I wanted the movie to show all that.

On the day they would be shooting the Halloween scenes, I awoke to an anxiety attack. I was going back down the rabbit hole. I knew I would have to pull myself up and be strong, so I got dressed, jumped into my car to drop Trentan off at the sitter's house, and met my mom at her house. Mom and I headed to Burbank, where the school scenes were to be shot that day. Later that afternoon, they would be filming the Halloween night scene, so Mom and I would make ourselves scarce.

Since we were in Burbank, Mom and I headed to IKEA, where we spent the better part of the afternoon as we waited for the director to call us back when they finished the scene. Unfortunately, there was a miscommunication and we were told to return too early. They had not wrapped up the scene, and as soon as the crew and actors saw us on the set, their faces all turned white. The director ran up to my mom and said, "Oh, Norma, we aren't quite done with the scene. Are you sure you want to stay?"

At this point, we were both tired from walking around IKEA for hours and just didn't want to leave. For the first time in a long time, I really had to keep my emotions in check because if I didn't, all hell would break loose, and I didn't think that would be fair to those around me.

I sat in the director's chair waiting for the scene of my mom and me arriving at the school that night, and I relived finding my dad's truck shot up and his half covered body. The actors and crew were aware that the scene being played out was real life and some of the people being portrayed were watching it unfold all over again. My gut was hurting as I watched them move through the scene. I probably looked a little ashen, and one of the crew saw that I didn't look well and got me something to calm my stomach.

As they wrapped up the scene, both Mom and I were relieved that the roller-coaster emotions were over for the day. Exhausted, we headed home.

As soon as I walked through the door, I scooped Trentan up into my arms, hugged him, and gave him a kiss. I was back to my happy place.

On January 17, 1994, the Northridge earthquake had just ripped through Southern California killing seventy-five people and causing billions of dollars in damage. Matt, Trentan, and I were living in a tiny apartment atop a hill in Santa Clarita, California, and we sustained some minor damage. Dishes had flown from the cupboards, landing on the floor and shattering everywhere and we lost our television set. After the cleanup, we attended the premier of the movie, *The Price of Vengeance*, which was part of the *In the Line of Duty* made-for-television movie series. It was our story.

We were excited to see the final product. I knew it would be hard to relive that night through the movie, but I felt it was important to take the whole experience in. As we sat in the audience and the lights went down, the music set the tone for the movie. I endured watching part of my life unfold on the screen, wondering if my dad would love or hate the movie.

At the end of the movie, they mentioned what had happened since the tragedy. They talked about the convictions and spoke of my mom being the president of Concerns of Police Survivors and how she lobbied against the sale of semiautomatic weapons. They displayed pictures of Ryan in his Police Explorer uniform and his desire to follow in his father's footsteps. That was how it ended. Once again, I felt my heart break as I realized that even after all of those years, I'd been left out just like when I was seventeen.

I wanted people to see that I was grown and married with a beautiful baby boy named after his grandfather. I sat there speechless remembering how I felt when people forgot that my dad had a daughter, as well as a wife and son, many years earlier. Talking through it with Matt on the ride home, I realized that I had the power to make things right, so I decided to reach out to the production company.

I had a conversation with the production company and was told that they would put my name in the credits at the end. That was not the acknowledgment I wanted about being a part of the story, and I felt defeated.

A couple of weeks after the premier, the movie was set to air on NBC. Unfortunately, we no longer had a television, thanks to the earthquake, so we would have to find another way to watch it. I didn't feel comfortable going to a bar with our son in tow, and most of the area bars had been damaged by the earthquake anyway, so we decided to go to Matt's business partner's condo to watch it on his television. But when we arrived, he told us that his television was broken too.

I was desperate, so I jumped out of my comfort zone and started to knock on doors at the condo complex. We knocked on a few doors but got no answer. Finally, as we we about to give up, a kind lady answered and listened to my crazy story as we stood on her doorstep. "You might think we're a little crazy," I said, "but there's a television movie about to be aired on NBC, and it is about something that happened to our family. Our televisions were broken in the earthquake. May we come in and watch it on your television?"

Much to our surprise, she invited us into her living room and turned on the television. It was scary to be watching it with a total stranger and letting her into my world. I had knots in my stomach, and she kept looking over at me and then back at the TV as if to say she could hardly believe this happened to our family. When the movie ended, we thanked her for her kindness and hugged her good-bye.

About a day after the movie aired, my phone began to ring. My friends wanted to know what I thought of the movie and why I wasn't mentioned at the end of it.

13

More Blessings

After the excitement of the movie was over and things started to get back to normal, I concentrated on my sweet son. When I was pregnant with Trentan, Matt and I took a child psychology class. I loved being a mom, but I was most thankful to the teacher of that class.

I really stressed about the kind of mom I wanted to be, and I wanted the history of abuse on my mom's side to stop with me. That would be the key to change according to our teacher. She reminded all of us in the class that we needed to leave all the past hurts behind and walk out the door with a different outlook on being a parent ourselves. My mom had grown up with an abusive, self-absorbed mother, so she really had no one to guide her as a mom. I chose the good things she taught me and put away the ones that hurt, shoving them deep so they wouldn't surface in my relationship with my child. I would chose to encourage my child, be honest with him, and help him through the hard days. I never wanted my kid to have a day when he felt emotionally abandoned by his mom.

Given everything I had gone through and the constant insecurity I was still living with, I didn't want my child to see and know my fear. My world was different now that I was a mom, and it was now my job and Matt's job to protect our child from the harsh realities of life.

Three years later, we added another child to our family when my sweet Dylan Taylor Snow was born. Trentan was excited to meet "his" baby. Now my family felt complete. We enjoyed every day with the kids, but I still had feelings of insecurity when it came to safety, and my fears of danger lurking were stronger now that I was a mom of two. Matt and I started to talk about moving away to a place where I would feel safer. When Trentan was a toddler, Matt and I took him with us to Denver, Colorado, to visit a friend who lived there, and we fell in love with the state. His parents were in Minnesota, but we both felt like the climate was too cold there. Denver would be the halfway point between both sides of the family, so visits would be easier.

The thought of moving to a state where no one knew my backstory brought me joy. I would lie in the bed at night visualizing us living in Denver, and I prayed for an opportunity to move there. I fantasized about the beautiful Colorado countryside, the Rocky Mountains, and schools that had greenery around them instead of huge fences. Colorado would be a better place to raise our kids.

That January, I was scheduled to work the Long Beach Hair Show as a platform artist teaching hair cutting techniques. I knew vendors from all parts of the United States would be there, and I prayed I would meet someone from Denver at the show. My excitement grew as I arrived at the Long Beach Convention Center. It was completely chaotic backstage as we were prepping our models, but as I worked, I had a conversation with one of the assistants about wanting to move to Denver. As I kept talking, I noticed a woman across the room listening to my conversation. Then she walked away, and I thought no more about it.

But before the show started, a man named Harry approached me saying he'd heard about me and my work. He invited me to meet with him and his wife about a business opportunity. I was too busy to give it any thought, so I stuck his business card into the pocket of my apron and told him I would call him on my break.

It was a busy and long day with so many models, and I felt like Janet Jackson onstage with a headset demonstrating techniques. I was exhausted but still managed to call Harry. We made plans to meet for coffee before I started the second day of the show. That night in my hotel room, I prayed to meet someone from Denver the next day.

The next morning, I met Harry at the coffee shop adjacent to the convention center. I shook his hand and met his wife. Harry told me he'd met a woman at the show the previous day who knew he was from Colorado Springs. She pointed me out and told him I wanted to move to Denver. After that casual meeting, he talked to my colleagues at the show, and they told him I was a top-notch hairdresser, colorist, educator, and platform artist.

My eyes had already gotten big, but when those last words came out of his mouth, I thought he was talking about someone else. I wasn't great about receiving compliments, so when I got them, I didn't know what to say.

"Susan, we own a beauty product distribution center based out of Colorado Springs, Colorado," he said. "We're looking for someone like you to take our top hair product line and grow our territory. We believe we can do it through education. We believe you are the one who can do that for us. We would like to offer you a position as our lead educator and sales associate in Denver, Colorado." He suggested a salary.

I was stunned. The offer was more than I was currently making, and we were struggling financially. It seemed a perfect solution, but I needed to think about Matt and his job. I told Harry and his wife that Matt was in construction and Harry jotted down the names of several companies on a napkin—companies where he had contacts. He thought he would be able to get Matt interviews with them.

I sat there gazing into their faces in total disbelief. My prayers were being answered and we were being blessed with an opportunity, despite the fact that I hadn't felt particularly faithful to God.

We ended the meeting with a hug instead of a handshake. I told them I needed to speak to Matt and I would get back to them the next day. I went on about my day excited with the conversation at the front of my mind, and I couldn't get back to my hotel fast enough at the end of the show to call Matt and tell him about my conversation with Harry and his wife.

Like me, Matt was excited about the opportunity to make our dream of living in Denver come true. Neither of us could believe our good luck in what had transpired. As soon as I got back from the show, we booked a flight to Denver to check things out with Harry. Matt could interview with some of the companies Harry had recommended while we were there. It was a short trip, and as soon as we returned to California, Matt received three offers of employment.

We were elated that things were starting to fall in place. We immediately found a home to rent and started to pack. Moving with boys four years and ten months old was a challenge, but being able to distance myself from the bad memories and pain trumped the inconvenience of moving to another state with small children.

We moved that April, and I had hope for the future. I was sure we could give our kids better memories than I'd had growing up.

14

Beginning a Journey

By the time I'd lived in Colorado for a couple of years, I felt life had finally turned the corner for me. I was moving forward in my grief journey. I believed I would be okay regardless of what life threw at me. I no longer felt unsafe and I no longer felt the anxiety tied to the memories of my old childhood home and neighborhood.

That all changed on April 20,1999. I was working in a salon in Greenwood Village, Colorado, just south of Denver. I had left my client in my chair to process her hair color and headed to the back break room. Out the slightly open back door, I could see it was a beautiful day. One of the other stylists had turned on our small television and a breaking news alert came on.

Two students had begun shooting students outside Columbine High School in Littleton, Colorado, another suburb of Denver. Then they entered the school and continued their shooting spree. I watched film of students coming out of the school in single file lines, hands in the air, passing ambulances and blaring police lights. I kept watching the scenes unfolding on the television and felt my legs start to give way beneath me. I fell down into the chair in front of the table where the television was set up.

Suddenly I had visions of the school where my dad was killed. I thought about the kids being locked down at Columbine, just like the kids at the school where my dad was killed. I started shaking and one of my coworkers looked at me with concern. "Do you know someone at that school?" she asked.

Oh no, I thought to myself. *Now I have to explain where this anxiety and trembling is coming from.* The problem was, I didn't understand it myself. I didn't know anyone at that school. Why was I trembling? And why was my stomach feeling sick? The fogginess I'd experienced after my dad died returned. My vision narrowed and my hearing began to fade—just as they would if I were about to pass out. I was watching the reporters filming teens as their world crumbled, their sense of safety and security evaporated, and their innocence was lost, just like I experienced at their age. My heart sickened.

In the days following the Columbine High School shootings, I was plagued by a deep sadness. I couldn't escape it no matter where I was or what I did. I just couldn't shake it off. Once again I felt hopeless. Once again I felt I was just going through the motions as I lived my life. I had fallen into that dark cavern again and was not seeing the light. It was an effort to get out of bed. I found myself struggling with being a wife and mother and with running my hair business.

Every day I went to the salon, put on a happy face, and tried to not let anyone know about the darkness I was swimming in. As soon as I left the salon and got into my car to drive home, I planned my death in my head. Should I just drive off the road on my way home? Should I take a bunch of pills when the kids were at school, fall asleep, and never wake up? I knew I couldn't deal with the deep sadness I felt during the day and the panic attacks that awakened me at night to find myself in a pool of sweat with a pounding heart, tingling hands, and a dry mouth. I was falling down a deep dark rabbit hole, and I had no idea how to climb out.

Matt watched me spiral down and felt helpless because neither one of us understood what was happening to me. Finally, he met me at the door one day when I arrived home. "Either you get some help or I'm putting you in a hospital!" he said.

He was right. I couldn't pretend everything was okay. My coworkers probably realized there was something going on with me but didn't want to say anything. I was scared to death. My depression was at its peak, and I felt crazy. Yet, even as one part of me contemplated death, another part of me understood that taking my own life would turn life upside-down for my husband and kids. I knew what it was like to go through life without a parent, and I didn't want my kids to grow up without their mom. I had no idea what I was dealing with and was anxious about embarking on a journey to deal with it, but I felt ready. And I didn't want my husband and kids to keep watching me spiraling downward.

I made an appointment with a local therapist. I was apprehensive because my previous experience in therapy was a disappointment. Part of that was on me because I had never told that therapist what was going on inside me. But some of it was on him too because he'd never asked questions that would allow me to be honest and open about my emotions. I was hopeful about this new therapist. I had to be.

My first appointment was going to be scary, but I was going to allow myself to be vulnerable and tell her everything. I promised Matt that I would be totally transparent about all the emotions I was feeling.

During my first session, my therapist said we were going to get to know one another and create a safe plan for me. I was amenable to whatever needed to be done, so I shared the story of my father's death and explained what had happened when I watched the coverage about the Columbine shootings. I told her about my depression, my thoughts of death, my panic attacks at night, the face I tried to put forward at work, and the roller-coaster ride I was on every day. I told her everything—including that I felt I was going crazy.

She listened intently and compassionately, and when I finished, she said, "You're experiencing post-traumatic stress disorder."

I couldn't believe what I was hearing. I wasn't crazy! I thought my head would explode. She told me that in time, I would actually start looking forward to my sessions with her.

I learned that while first responders—those in the military, police, firefighters, paramedics, doctors, and nurses—do sometimes have PTSD, anyone who has experienced trauma may have the disorder. She explained that when a person experiences trauma, the brain is damaged and starts to rewire itself. It goes into protection mode, and sometimes it tucks the traumatic experiences deep inside the brain. So when I saw my dad at the scene that night, my brain tucked it away. The fogginess was my brain's way of protecting me.

She explained that when someone has PTSD, the physiological response to the trauma may also lead to anxiety, depression, and bipolar disorder. According to her, most people with PTSD will also experience a co-occurring mental disorder over the course of their life.

We talked about how the trauma I endured in my teens had just been tucked away for the time being. It was like a ticking time bomb waiting to explode one day. The Columbine shootings had triggered that explosion, and all the emotions erupted at once. She described it as being like a tsunami coming toward me. That's exactly how it felt: a giant wave of emotions sweeping me up, taking my sense of self away, and leaving me with emptiness and darkness again.

She said that while PTSD was something I would always deal with, she would give me some tools to help me navigate it. I had been suffering in silence for a long time, and now that was over. It was a relief to know I could learn how to manage my emotions better when something triggered me.

That was my first lesson: my triggers. Learning your triggers is the hardest part to get through. "Usually you have to go to the memory of that traumatic experience to understand your trigger," she said. "Most people won't want to do that because to do so, they have to relive that moment in their life."

One of the first things she had me do was journal. She asked me to journal whatever I was thinking and feeling every day, even if those thoughts and feelings were dark. She explained that it was a way to free my brain from holding on to the thoughts, allowing them to fester.

We began each therapy session going over my journals. That was hard. It meant I had to be vulnerable with another person.

The second lesson was to not only be honest with her but also with Matt. I had spent many years sheltering him from what lived in my head. I pretended to be okay when I wasn't. I felt shame in speaking about my emotions with anyone because I didn't want to burden them with my problems. Even when I had panic attacks, I went to a place where no one could see me suffering. I didn't want people to think I was crazy.

During one session, she told me to describe in detail the night my dad was killed. My fingers tingled, I started to sweat, and my heart pounded. I struggled with allowing myself to move through the anxiety attack I was experiencing. I kept telling her I felt I was dying and wanted to stop.

When I started to hyperventilate in fear, she said, "Happy place. Visualize a place where you feel at peace, a place where you feel happy."

I moved away from the school scene and toward a beautiful visual of white sand beaches. I focused on palm trees swaying in the wind and the faint sound of the water crashing against the shore. My breathing and heartbeat slowed, the tingling left my fingers, and I felt at peace.

Tears started rolling down my cheeks and I grabbed a tissue from the table by my chair to wipe them.

"I just taught you how to ground yourself when you feel out of control," she said.

I wished I had been taught the grounding technique years earlier.

We continued to work on grounding techniques for the next month of sessions. Unfortunately, anxiety wasn't the only issue I dealt with. I also suffered from depression, and it was not only the biggest issue, it was the hardest for me because dark thoughts accompanied it. I was learning how to ground myself, and I was hopeful I could also learn how to manage depression.

The doctor had put me on an antidepressant, and it was helping to manage the hills and valleys of my emotions. But I still needed another way to get through the bouts of darkness I was experiencing. Shame reared its head with the depression because I felt I was letting my husband and kids down. I also felt bad for not being a better daughter to my mom and sister to my brother. I barely knew how to navigate life myself, but I was remorseful for not being a better person for the people I loved most. I admitted to the therapist that I had thoughts of leaving them all to be with my dad in heaven.

I thought I was weak for not figuring out how to just feel better, and some friends even told me to get over it because my dad had been gone for a long time. I was frustrated that I didn't have a life in which I wholeheartedly felt complete and happy, but there was shame in having those thoughts too. I wanted to feel love with everything I had, but I always felt there was a limit to what I could feel. People told me how strong I was, and I thought I needed to keep up that façade or people would lose faith in me.

My therapist reminded me that I had been a teenager when the trauma of my dad's death occurred, and I hadn't been mature enough to understand what loving wholeheartedly felt like then. I'd been going through my life in fight, flight, or freeze mode for so many years that I needed to understand my emotions before I could heal from the things that had hurt me. Strength came from being able to be vulnerable, she said.

We started to dive into all the emotions I'd felt throughout my life, one by one. Along with the therapy, I read books about PTSD to understand the emotional responses to different traumas, and I learned many things. It was a relief to understand there is no shame in having PTSD. The brain is a powerful machine, and when trauma occurs, the amygdala, hippocampus, and prefrontal cortex are all negatively impacted. The only way to manage it is to be being willing to move through emotional pain.

One of the books I read talked about different therapies used to heal PTSD, and EMDR (eye movement desensitizing and reprocessing) was one of those therapies. It seemed a little out there to me at first. With EMDR, one of several techniques—including tapping, eye movement, tones, and electric pulses—could be used when the patient was asked to recall distressing images. I talked it over with my therapist, but I was just getting used to talk therapy, and I decided it might be something to do later on. Therapy, books, and an antidepressant seemed to be working. I had more control over my emotions.

By allowing myself to be vulnerable, my therapist could look deep into my soul and help me learn to fight my pain. Healing would be work, and it would be the fight of my life to get my life back on track. Before meeting my new therapist, I had no idea what a trigger was, and I was thankful to learn about them from her and from the books I was reading on PTSD. For me, songs like "Amazing Grace" played on bagpipes or sounds like a gun salute or the bugling of "Taps" were triggers. Visual triggers included the sight of a flag-draped coffin or certain images I saw on the news. Even smells could be a trigger. When I experienced one of these triggers, I went into panic mode because they took me back to the traumatic experience of my dad's killing.

For the first time, I was finally starting to understand how the trauma had been affecting me, and while I found facing my trauma difficult, I knew it was necessary. I was more confident moving forward because I had some tools to help me cope with triggers, but I wasn't fooling myself into thinking I could handle *everything*. I knew I would be tested.

On Sept 11, 2001 another tragic event happened. I had just dropped my kids off at school and was getting ready to head to the salon when I turned on the television for a bit. The morning news was interrupted with breaking news. I watched a plane fly into the World Trade Center, and moments later, another plane hit the other World Trade Center tower. Anxiety started in my chest and worked its way to my brain, and I became overwhelmed with the feeling that I was no longer safe.

I thought about my sweet, innocent kids sitting in their classroom, unaware of what was happening in their world. I wasn't experiencing any flashbacks, but the anxiety was real. I wanted to go to the school and scoop up my kids, but I hesitated because I didn't want them to see me in the anxious state I was in. I prayed to God to take the panic away. Then I remembered the coping skills I'd learned from my therapist. I took deep breaths, and as I let them out, I envisioned my happy place, the beach. I visualized the water and felt the warm wind against my face.

At work, my phone rang with calls from upset clients canceling their appointments for the day. The world felt changed, and I couldn't tear myself from the television coverage. I wanted to stay away but just couldn't. I watched the towers collapse and all that was lost. I felt the emotions of the people running from the collapsing buildings and felt their helplessness. I watched police officers run into the buildings and knew my dad would have done the same thing. I felt the pain of all the families who had lost loved ones that day and realized that once again my world had been turned upside down. But this time, it wasn't just me. It was everyone around me too. This time I didn't feel alone on an island in my sadness. It was a reminder that life is precious, and I didn't want to waste my life giving my emotions power over me.

I started to journal again. I had many insecurities about what had occurred, but I wasn't going to allow myself to be engulfed. I talked to friends and family about the September 11 events, and I was open about how I felt. I started each day in gratitude for the beautiful family I was blessed with. I looked for and saw the good in people to remind myself that there was hope for me and all humans.

15

The Carpet Is Ripped Out from Under Me

After the loss of my dad, I believed nothing that bad would ever happen to me again. I was wrong.

I had spent many years building a relationship with Matt's family, and they were the "normal" in my life. Matt's mom and dad had been supportive and loving from the start of our relationship. His dad, Larry, was the one I went to for advice on things like finances and business issues. He had a green thumb I was always jealous of, he was the king of sticky notes describing where things went and how they worked, and he made me laugh as he followed the kids around the house with a vacuum when they were little. Matt's mom was sweet and quiet. She was the Martha Stewart of the family when it came to creativity. I could be silly with her, but she also listened when I needed someone to talk to. I felt at home with Matt's family.

Larry had fought cancer as a young man and had some health issues. Back then, the treatments were harsher, and they wreaked havoc on his insides. He died at sixty-one on Christmas Eve, 2001. Another dad lost. My heart was torn apart watching Matt have to say good-bye to his dad. His family meant the world to him, and losing his dad changed him.

I thought I could help Matt the way he'd helped me many years earlier, but I watched him pull away. He had always been flirtatious with other women, and I made excuses about it. I told myself he was just joking. As our relationship began deteriorating, I pretended everything was fine and we were just going through a rough spot. We were considered the perfect couple, and I didn't want that moniker tarnished, so I just pretended our marriage was great. After all, we seldom fought.

During spring break of 2004, we decided to go to Minnesota to see Matt's family. He was being distant, and I hoped getting away would do us some good. Also, Larry had been gone for two years, and I thought it would be good to see his mom and sisters. Money was tight, so we decided to drive. During the road trip, I had a sense that Matt was troubled about something. He seemed anxious. I knew that being at the house without his dad would be hard on him, but it felt like more than that. Something seemed to be weighing heavy on his heart, but he wasn't letting me in to know what it was.

I could see he was trying to put on a happy face as we pulled into the driveway at his parents' house. It was like the façade I put on when I didn't want people to see my pain.

After the excited hellos with his mom and sisters, he let the kids stay in the house while we went out to the porch. "I met someone," he blurted out. "Her name is Regan." What he was actually saying to me didn't register at first. Then he told me they had been sleeping together, and a flood of past experiences with other women came flying out of his mouth.

I fell onto the porch bench. My brain was having a hard time taking in everything he was saying. I sat there in total disbelief that the one person who truly knew my heart had just shattered it in a five-minute conversation. I was devastated. My life felt over. Why would he do that to us? Many emotions flooded my mind, and I felt lost. What was I going to say to our kids and his family?

I left the porch, went directly upstairs to the room we were supposed to sleep in, and asked Matt give his family some excuse so they would leave me alone. I couldn't believe Matt would betray our marriage. He'd said he met the woman at our son's school, and I wondered what kind of woman was willing to break up a family. Anger flooded my body. Then sadness. Then anger again. I was on a roller coaster of emotions.

I spent three days in the room not wanting to see or talk to anyone. Matt's family figured out that we were not in a good way and just let us do whatever we needed to. They took care of the kids and kept them busy as much as possible. Depression had hit me in the worst way, and I couldn't let my kids see me in that state of mind. The only time I came out of the room was when my mother-in-law, Marcia, let us know that a photographer had arrived to take family photos. I grappled with my sadness as I sat on the bedroom floor trying to hide the dark circles under my eyes with makeup, put a little blush on my pale cheeks, and run a brush through my hair.

I put on a fake smile and joined the rest of the family for photos. I had to dig deep to find the strength to pretend to be a family when I knew it had been torn apart. After the photo shoot was done, I couldn't take it anymore and went back to the bedroom. I wanted to get on a plane and return to Colorado, but I didn't want to disappoint the kids. So I stayed for the two days we had left.

Back on the road, I had thirteen hours of stewing in my emotions while I sat next to the man who'd just broken my heart. I wanted to make him hurt too, so I played all the songs that reminded us of better times. We drove in silence. Even the kids were silent. I knew they must have realized something was wrong, but they didn't ask questions.

When we finally arrived home, I didn't bother taking out any luggage. I just sent the kids to their rooms so Matt and I could talk in our bedroom. I could see the remorse and sadness in his eyes as we sat on the small chaise near the window and talked. My dad wouldn't have given up, and neither was I. We talked about marriage therapy. Matt told me the woman he was having the affair with had been watching our cat while we were away, and I demanded that he get our key from her. He agreed and said he would end things with her.

His words told me he didn't want the marriage to end and would work on it with me. I was hopeful he was telling me the truth. After all, we'd been together for more than eighteen years, and that was too long to just throw it all away.

He left the house to get the key, but he wasn't gone long before he came back in and met me in the living room. "I want a divorce," he said.

I looked up to see my kids staring down from the hallway near their rooms. They both screamed, and I sunk down on the floor. The room started to spin as I realized my family was now broken and there was no going back. I wondered what the hell had happened. Surely, he couldn't love her the way he loved me.

The next couple of days were rough. I couldn't understand what had gone wrong. Matt's mom came to town once he told her what was happening. She wanted to help with the kids because she knew they would be devastated. They were both very angry with their dad, and I wasn't in the mindset to say the right things to make them feel better.

Something was eating at me, so when Marcia decided to get out of the house for a few minutes, I called Matt at work. After some talk about the kids, I got down to what was bothering me. "Is Regan pregnant?"

The line grew silent. Then he quietly said the words I wasn't prepared to hear. "Yes. She's pregnant."

There was a crack in the universe. I must have let out a loud scream because my mother-in-law raced down the street to the house as fast as she could. When I met her at the door, I told her the news. She immediately gave me a long hug and started to apologize.

I backed out of the embrace and looked at her. "It's not your fault! *He* chose to do this to us!"

Immediately, I went to the bedroom and gathered all of Matt's stuff from our closet and threw the items on the floor. Marcia came upstairs with a trash bag and helped me stuff his clothes in the bags. It felt as if I were throwing away my future, my happiness, and the world I was used to. I really didn't know how to do life without Matt.

The next couple of days were spent trying to get support for my kids at their school. Making sure my kids would get through the breakup was my priority, so I stuffed my own hurt and anger and continued to do what I could to protect them and give them an outlet for their thoughts and emotions.

I remembered how important it was to talk out my own thoughts with my therapist, so I decided to give them that opportunity at home and also in family counseling, which Matt agreed to. The counseling office was a safe place to tell Matt how they were feeling, and Matt was able to hear them there.

I spent a lot of time trying to be the best I could be even though I was completely empty inside. It wasn't healthy. I stuffed my emotions without realizing the damage I was causing myself. My body was shutting down from normal functioning because my brain was processing so much emotion at a high rate. I was anxious and couldn't sleep. Because I had no appetite, I dropped weight quickly, and in my mind, that was a good thing. Unfortunately, I found myself spiraling downward both outwardly and internally. I was returning to my old habits of taking everything on myself and having a hard time asking for help.

After a conversation with the kids one night, I lay in bed thinking about my life and realized that I needed to take stock of myself. Instead of buying in to the idea that Matt had single-handedly caused the demise of our marriage, I sat up, walked up to the bedroom mirror, and stared deeply at my reflection. I didn't like who was staring back. I wasn't the person I'd been telling myself I was.

I started to journal about my contributions to the marriage, both good and bad. I realized that I hadn't treated the marriage as a partnership. I'd stopped believing in myself and my worth, and I knew it wasn't only Matt who had been absent in the marriage. I hadn't been completely present either. I'd put others before him and taken him for granted.

I stopped blaming him and starting taking ownership for the mistakes I'd made in our relationship. It wasn't a pretty road. I wrote down all the attributes I wanted in a loving relationship, and I wrote about what I wanted my life to look like for myself. I read books about divorce.

The one thing that had always made me feel more in control of my life was educating myself with information and tools I could use to help me navigate life. I peeled away layers of denial about my marriage and saw that I'd spent a lot of time pretending everything in our marriage was fine. I'd spent a lot of time holding on to a relationship with problems we never addressed. I had lived in a fantasy that my marriage was going to last forever and that Matt would be in love with me forever.

Every day, I looked in the mirror, reminding myself that I didn't like the person I'd been before my marriage collapsed. And it was up to me to become the person I needed to be to be a better partner and a better mom for my kids.

After a few months of reading books and being in individual and family therapy, I realized that I was still going to find a way to be friends with Matt so we could co-parent in a healthy way. But being a friend was going to be hard for me because I still missed being married.

I noticed that Matt was dropping weight, and his skin color looked ashen. He didn't look healthy, and his eyes were bloodshot every time he came to the house to pick up the kids. I stepped outside my own suffering long enough to see that he was suffering too. Others told me I shouldn't care about how he felt and that he deserved to be miserable, and while there were days when I agreed with them in the beginning, I moved past my anger and hurt. I didn't like seeing my friend spiral down.

It was time for me to do something healthy for myself and for him. I sat down at the table and grabbed one of Trentan's notebooks from school. My hand shook as the words I had been holding back from saying started oozing out of my brain. I told Matt about taking a close look at myself and taking responsibility for the mistakes I'd made in our marriage. I wrote about the person I wanted to be. I said that he seemed unhappy with the direction his life was taking. I reminded him that for years, he had tried to do what would bring happiness but that happiness seemed to be eluding him. I encouraged him to peel away the layers of himself internally to find what he wanted for his life and future relationships.

I waited three days and reread the letter before I finally stuck it in an envelope and sent it to him at work. I knew he might read it and consider my words or read it and tell me to go to hell. I needed to accept how he took it and not be attached to an outcome. I had spoken my truth for the first time in years. I'd finally been honest with both him and myself.

There was a release in doing that.

16

Endings and Beginnings

Matt and I were both headed to California, but we had separate itineraries. I was taking the boys to see my mom and he was taking Regan, his new companion, to his twentieth high school reunion. It was hard for me to not be a part of that event since we were both good friends with his high school friends, but I knew it was going to be nice spending some quality time with my kids.

Mom picked us up at the airport, and as we made our way through the San Fernando Valley, memories of the places Matt and I had been to together came flooding into my head. We had so much history there, and I couldn't just wipe that history from my memory. Tears welled up and began to stream down my face.

My mom looked over at me and said, "Susan, don't let the kids see you upset."

I slumped down in my seat feeling hollow and defeated inside. The support I needed was not there.

As soon as we arrived at the time share my mom owned in Ventura, I got the kids settled and we headed to the pool for some fun. As I was just about to sit down near the pool, my cell phone rang. It was Matt calling, and my heart skipped a little. I answered the phone expecting him to ask for the kids. Instead, he asked me how I was doing, how the flight had been, and what the time share was like. Some part of me waited for him to ask me to join him at his reunion, but that invitation didn't come, even though I could tell from his voice that he was thinking about it.

When his friend entered the room and asked who he was talking to, he immediately asked to talk to the kids. When the call was over, I wondered what it had meant. Was he having a bad time with her?

I had been the one to file for divorce, and the divorce was final on July 4, less than three months later. I had accepted the end of our marriage and didn't know what the future would hold, but for the first time in months, I was ready to approach life differently and allow myself to date. I had written down everything I wanted in a mate. It was the first time I'd allowed myself to think about someone other than Matt fitting my list.

The first day back from the California trip was the day I had to give the kids up to Matt for the day. He was excited to see them when he came to pick them up. The kids were happy to spend time with him, and their grandma had given them money before they left California, so they wanted Matt to take them to the store to spend it.

I was planning to relax with a book at home while the kids were with their dad, but when Matt called, he sounded frantic. He'd just had a horrible fight with Regan. It began when he ran into her at Target. She wanted to hang out with him and our kids, but Matt wanted to have time alone with the kids. An argument ensued and Matt fled to the parking lot with our kids in tow.

When they drove off, she followed him, weaving in and out of traffic to keep up with him. They finally pulled over, and he said he'd gone over to her car to ask her to leave him and the kids alone. The conversation had become heated, and he'd broken up with her right there in the parking lot of our church. She went running after him when he returned to his truck, and when he got in, she'd ripped open the back passenger side door where our son was sitting. His immediate response was to drive off to safety, leaving her in a cloud of dust as he dashed away.

I could hear that he was scared, and I heard the kids crying in the background. All I could do in that moment was to put my anger aside and tell Matt that he should go to our friends' house, let the kids decompress, and give himself some time to get himself together for both his sake and the sake of the kids.

I wanted to run to my kids and protect them, but I knew Matt would have to handle the situation. When he brought the kids home, we decided to seek help through the school to support the kids through this latest trauma. It was the best thing we could do for them and for us as a family.

It was a rough week. I had plans to go to a Beastie Boys concert Saturday night with a guy I was seeing, but he called on

Thursday to tell me he couldn't go to the concert. It felt like the universe was telling me to invite Matt, and even though I was nervous, I called to invite him. He loved the Beastie Boys, and I knew we would enjoy the concert. To my surprise, he accepted my invitation.

I was nervous the night of the concert, but I went into the experience with no expectations. It was just two friends going to a concert. He looked happy when I picked him up at the house he was staying at, and he smelled so good, it took me back to when we first met. He might have been feeling the same way because he complimented me on my outfit as soon as he got into the car.

We talked at the concert, and while the concert was great, our conversation was even better. Something felt familiar but different between us. He was more attentive than he'd ever been. We laughed and danced, but as we left the concert, anxiety returned. I didn't want to tell him how I was feeling, so I concentrated on driving and kept my thoughts to myself.

Thoughts and feelings swirled within me on my drive home after dropping him off. Could I still be in love with him? I'd convinced myself that we would never be together again, but now I was confused.

The next day, I talked to a good friend about the concert and how it felt to be with Matt. "You need to tell Matt the truth about what you were feeling," he said. He told me I shouldn't wait, that I should call Matt to see if we could meet for lunch that day.

Even though I was apprehensive, I called Matt, and he agreed to meet me for lunch. With butterflies in my stomach and sweaty palms, I drove to pick him up. At the restaurant, we sat without saying anything until I mustered the courage to talk. I told him about how I'd felt the night before and explained that I had no expectations. I could see that the conversation was making him nervous, but I just needed to get my feelings off my chest.

He sat back in his chair and looked into my eyes. "I felt the same things you were feeling. I made all the people in that concert go away and paid attention to everything you were saying. I couldn't believe I hadn't noticed how much I enjoyed just talking with you."

I didn't know what to say. Where did we go from there? His revelation was exciting, but at the same time, I was terrified.

After that day, we spent many weekends together with the kids. As friends at first. I was afraid to let myself love him again, and I didn't want our kids to know how we felt.

But I didn't realize that the universe had bigger plans for us.

17

Reconciliation

About a month later, Matt moved into an apartment by himself. He spent time with us after work, but neither of us allowed ourselves to give into our feelings for one another.

One day we were both invited to a mutual friend's party. Our kids were friends with theirs, so we had hung out together when Matt and I were still married. I wasn't going to stay at the party for too long because I had plans that night to go out with a friend.

Something felt different when I saw him at the party. We found ourselves actually flirting with each other, and I didn't think we could hold back our feelings. Even our friends noticed the energy between us. I had walked over to our friends' house for the party, and when it was time for me to head back to my house to get ready for the evening, I made my way to the kitchen to tell our friends good-bye. I caught Matt's eye, and he quickly came over to offer a ride to my house.

"Sure," I said.

When we got to the house, instead of dropping me off, he asked to come in and hang out with me for a while. I left him in the living room and went upstairs to my room to grab something, and as I came out of my closet, I saw that Matt was standing in the bedroom. My heart raced as he pulled me close and kissed me. I knew that what was happening between us would complicate things but neither of us could hold back our feelings.

After our encounter, he got dressed and left to go back to the party. I asked myself what I'd just done. I wondered where this was going and if I could trust him with my heart again.

Without skipping a beat, we began dating, and we attempted to do so without the kids knowing about it, though we didn't succeed at that. My heart was still healing and I was still working on finding a way through grief and trauma. It was all too much for me. We decided to go into therapy as a couple to help us navigate everything we were going through to heal the relationship and create a different, more healthy path together. We openly communicated about everything that was different about our current relationship from how it had been in the past—both the good and the bad.

On one of our dates at his apartment, we decided to rent a movie after dropping the kids off with friends. We sat on his lumpy couch and watched *The Passion of the Christ*. It wasn't really a date night kind of movie, but something had drawn me to it. The movie triggered many thoughts and feelings for me, and I sobbed watching it. It didn't take long for Matt to join me with his tears.

Jesus had endured great pain, and yet he forgave those who were putting him to death. I slid down to the floor as if something in my body had given out. If Jesus could forgive, so could I. I looked at Matt with tears in my eyes and said, "I'm going to forgive Lago for what he did to my family." And in another breath I said, "And I forgive you."

Matt dropped down to the floor, put his arms around me, and held me as we both cried. It was a turning point in my journey through both traumas. A giant weight had been lifted when those words came out of my mouth. But I also understood that with forgiveness came a great responsibility to honor myself and not allow others to influence my feelings about the subjects of my forgiveness. I wasn't forgetting Lago's horrific act. I was just taking back my power. I wasn't forgetting Matt's mistakes and infidelity. But I wasn't going to let anger and resentment damage the foundation of a relationship we were creating together.

I also had to find forgiveness for the woman who played a part in breaking up my family. She was carrying Matt's child, and because I had allowed myself to enter into this new relationship with him, I knew that both the child and the mother would be in my world.

I learned a lot about myself during the next few months. I discovered that many people didn't agree with my thoughts about forgiveness, and they saw their perceptions as being more important than mine. I lost friends and even some hair clients over my decision to forgive.

I came to understand that forgiveness was looked on as taboo by some people. But the only way I could heal from the trauma and move forward was to dig deep and forgive the people who had hurt me. That lesson did not come easily. It took delving deeply into myself and discovering what kind of person I wanted to be and what kind of relationships I wanted to have.

If I wanted to be truly happy, I was the one that needed to find the happiness within myself. The only way I could do that was through forgiveness. I wasn't forgetting all of the traumatic things that had happened. That would have been impossible. But I was giving myself grace. While I understood that some people saw forgiveness as giving power to the trauma and the people involved in it, I had discovered that for me, forgiveness was a path to *taking back* my power.

Where my marriage was concerned, I had to learn to forgive myself for allowing it to continue for so long when I knew at a deep level that Matt wasn't in it wholeheartedly. At a deep level, I had come to know that I deserved a man who would love me unconditionally. In fact, I deserved unconditional love from anyone I allowed to be important in my life, both friends and family.

I didn't see forgiveness as negating bad behavior. It didn't. But I didn't want to live my life with hate in my heart because I saw how that had affected my mother and brother as time went on after my dad's death.

In forgiveness, I also found vulnerability within myself. When I spoke to others about my dad's murder, some said, "Never forgive the men who took your dad's life," and when

Matt and I split, some people said, "A cheater is always a cheater." There was harshness in both of those comments. They were admonitions to be tough and avoid making myself vulnerable. But toughness and stoicism were of little help. Allowing myself to be vulnerable was.

It was easier to forgive Matt because he was remorseful from the beginning, and he was willing to dive deeply within himself to uncover what had motivated his behavior. But I'd never heard expressions of remorse from any of the men involved in the killing of my dad. When the remorse wasn't there, it was harder for me to forgive. But I knew that if I didn't find a way to forgive them, I would never heal. And I wasn't going to do that to myself. I finally began to unshackle myself from past traumas when I gave myself the gift of forgiveness.

I also had to work on forgiving myself for my own shortcomings. I'd spent a lot of time in victimhood, but I began to feel what it was like to be a survivor.

I needed forgiveness from my children because I knew they were riding the trauma from their parents' split and the challenges of our new relationship. Matt and I both needed to show the kids that while life can hand you some really hard situations, you can move through them and learn from them. I wanted to teach them about forgiveness early on in their lives so they wouldn't have the burden of holding on to anger and hate.

I wanted to live my life with love and forgiveness, and that was the legacy I wanted to leave my children.

Matt and me

18

Birth and New Beginning

Matt and I made sure the kids knew that even though he was having a baby with Regan, their feelings would still be a priority. As time grew closer to the baby's arrival, we both began to feel nervous and excited about meeting the new child. But on the other side of that emotion was fear. Fear crept in every time we thought of what it was going to be like to raise the child with Regan involved. Would we be able to co-parent? I contemplated being involved when the child was not mine, but to my surprise, every time I thought about that sweet little baby, I felt connected.

Daniel was born the beginning of March, and while I was excited about the birth, when Matt left for the hospital, I struggled with jealousy that he would be sharing this moment with her. As I watched him back out of the driveway, my cell phone rang. He wanted to reassure me that he was only going to meet his son and was not there for anything else. He said he was committed to our growing relationship.

The days following Daniel's birth were really hard. Regan had made no bones about the fact that she was unhappy with our reconciliation, and she appeared to be trying to manipulate Matt when it came to seeing his son. Six months after Daniel's birth, not only did we start going back to therapy to learn how to handle the co-parenting, we also found ourselves in the middle of a court battle with Regan because she didn't want Daniel to have anything to do with me.

Deep within my heart, all that mattered was Daniel. Many nights I lay awake wondering what he was like. I wanted to hold him. I was confused about my feelings because many people told me they didn't understand why I was accepting of the child my husband had fathered with another woman. I heard that I should not find forgiveness for the woman who had broken up my family, but deep within me, I knew she had only played a part in it and the biggest parts belonged to Matt and me.

Something inside me told me this beautiful child was sent here for a purpose. I looked at the situation, and as ugly as it could get at times, all I could do was love Daniel and think of the joy this sweet baby boy would bring to my family.

We were finally able to bring him to our home when Daniel was six months old, and I was excited to finally see his sweet little face in person. The anticipated visit was a long time coming, and we knew the court appointed advocate would be with Matt and baby Daniel when they came to the house.

I was at the house finishing cleaning up when I heard Matt entering through the front door. He carried the car seat with Daniel, who stared at me with the biggest eyes. Behind Matt was the court advocate. I followed them both into the living room. Matt set down the car seat with Daniel wrapped in a soft blanket. The advocate took a seat on the couch and watched me as I knelt down next to the car seat and began to sob. Matt took Daniel out of the seat, and Daniel reached out to me as I took him into my arms.

He started to cry as I gently squeezed him and rocked him to soothe his anxiety. "Hi, little man," I said with tears streaming down my face. "I've been waiting so long to meet and hold you. Welcome to the family, sweet boy."

My reaction confused the advocate, but I didn't care. Matt stood there watching me, and I think he was in shock seeing me like that with his son. I couldn't believe it myself. I actually felt the same way I had when our other boys were born. I felt joy! I felt my family was complete. Even though it was a rough road to get there, I felt blessed to have a third child in my life.

Not long after my introduction to Daniel, Matt and I started to talk about marriage again. This time, we wanted to do it right. It was important to both of us to teach our boys that even when things don't work out the way you think they will, you can learn from your mistakes and create a better and healthier relationship. We knew we had something extremely special in our relationship. Both of us had developed stronger selves, and we were finally honest with each other about everything.

In August of 2005, we had planned a trip to Minnesota to see Matt's family. Our divorce had taken a toll on them as well. We were excited to see them and let them see the new and improved relationship we had created that was based on truth and honesty, as well as love and forgiveness.

Before leaving for Minnesota we had another custody hearing. In a moment of pettiness, I decided to buy a fake engagement ring and wear it to the hearing. The ring I chose was too big, so I needed to get a ring guard to help it fit better. I went to a jewelry store a couple of days before the hearing to get one, but when I was there, I also looked at engagement rings and found a few I liked.

As we left to meet with friends the night before the hearing, I told Matt I needed to stop at the jewelry store for the ring guard. When we got to the jewelry store, Matt came in with me.

"Show me the rings you were looking at the other day," he said.

Matt always loved his sister's canary-yellow diamond ring, and that was the type of ring he wanted me to have the second time around. He asked the clerk if they had canary-yellow diamond rings and was told they didn't. So he asked me to show him the rings I'd looked at earlier.

I took his hand and led him to the case with the engagement rings, and the sales person brought out all the rings I'd looked at. "I want you to have something special," he said.

The sales person asked what kind of ring I was looking for.

"She wants a princess cut with white gold band," he replied. "I want her to have a canary yellow diamond."

"Wait a minute," the clerk said. "I might have the perfect ring for you."

She slipped away to the back and came back holding a ring. We couldn't believe it. She was holding a white gold ring with a canary-yellow diamond and two white diamonds on either side of the main diamond.

"It's my ring," I said excitedly. And it was. It looked perfect on my finger.

We handed it back to the sales lady and left with giant smiles on our faces.

I woke up the next morning with mixed feelings about what the day would hold. It was the day we would go to court for our custody hearing. Matt jumped out of bed and turned to me to say he needed to run some errands. I looked at his phone and saw he had looked at the jewelry store's hours. Could he be going back for the ring? It was exciting to think he might propose when we were in Minnesota with his family.

That afternoon, we needed to talk with our attorney before entering the hearing. He told us we needed to meet in a private room to go over our testimony, so we entered a tiny room. As I talked to the attorney, her eyes got big and she screamed, "What are you doing?"

She was looking at Matt, so I turned to see him on one knee. In his hand was a small black velvet-lined box with my ring. "Will you do me the honor of marrying me again?" he asked.

I was in a state of shock. I hadn't thought he would ask me to marry him there. I looked into Matt's eyes and said, "Yes!" as our attorney looked on tearfully.

No need for the fake ring. I was wearing the real one, and I was excited for my future. We beamed as we walked through the courtroom doors. Nothing that happened in that hearing was going to faze us. We had this!

Things started to calm down after the hearing, so we decided to plan the wedding. We chose August 5, 2006 to remarry.

Our first wedding had been planned by my mom and me, and it got away from me in the process. This time, the planning needed to be done by Matt and me. We wanted it to be *our* day and agreed to a small wedding. It was important for us to be surrounded by the friends and family who were a part of our relationship's healing journey, and we didn't want anything too traditional.

We spent many nights talking about the things that meant a lot to both of us, including the music. Music was healing for both of us, and we wanted our music to tell the story of our love for one another. This time, we wanted the children to be a part of the ceremony and reception. Trentan was thirteen and loved to bake, so we asked him to make some delicious cherry infused chocolate wedding cupcakes. We created our own menu, and the kids, with help from a family member, were able to help prepare the fresh barbecued vegetables and chicken main dish. This was an important healing for us, and it was important to do things as a family.

I awoke to bright blue skies on my wedding day. The wedding was going to take place in the backyard of my mother's new home with the backdrop of Pike's Peak in the distance.

And we were blessed to have Matt's mother and sister come into town from Minnesota for the wedding.

This time around, I was calm as I contemplated that this was the day we would commit our love. Matt had stayed at a friend's house, and as I sat in my robe by our bedroom window, he texted me. He just wanted me to know that he was still working on his vows and said he was looking forward to marrying me again. Warmth enveloped me, and I knew I was doing the right thing.

I went to the salon I worked at for my hair and makeup, and by the time I arrived at my mom's house, it had clouded up and was starting to rain. I sat in my mom's room waiting before it was time to dress, and even though people kept coming in to tell me it was raining hard, I continued to feel calm. Whatever the weather was doing, Matt and I were getting married. And I reminded myself that in Colorado, the weather could change drastically within fifteen minutes. The wedding was to start at 5:00 p.m. By 4:45, the rain had stopped and the clouds were beginning to part.

When I heard a soft knock on the bedroom door, I opened it up to find my oldest son, Trentan, standing there waiting to walk me down the aisle. He took my hand and led me to the slider door entrance to the backyard where all the people we loved who had helped and supported us through our journey sat. I saw the sweet face of little Daniel, now seventeen months old, staring back at me in the arms of his brother, Dylan. And as I thought back to the first wedding and how different this one felt, Trentan leaned in. "I love you, Mom," he whispered in my ear. Those words made my heart swell.

The music began to play. Trentan grabbed my arm, and we stepped onto the grass aisle. I could feel light rain caress my face, but I kept my gaze on Matt's eyes. The energy between us was palpable, and this time, it wasn't nervous energy.

Matt reached out to take my hand and Trentan hugged his dad. It was a sweet moment that brought tears to Matt's eyes. Standing side by side, we turned to one another and giggled when the pastor told us to look longingly into each other's eyes. He told our story of healing and forgiveness, and all three of us—Matt, me, and the pastor—teared up. I was really trying to keep it together so I would be able to recite my vows to Matt without losing it.

We vowed to respect each other, never take each other for granted, and always be honest. As those words were coming from our lips, I looked up for a brief moment to see a perfect rainbow in the distance. We knew that it was both of our dads telling us they were there celebrating our union in heaven.

We had been through hell and back, and we agreed that nothing could take that away from us. This was a clean start to a new marriage, and we were hopeful about our future together as a family.

Part 2
My Journey of Growth

19

My Journey of Growth Continues

We all have challenges in life, and some of us experience traumas that cause PTSD. But would I roll back the clock and change things if I could? The answer is no.

I have grown into the person I am today and I'm growing into the person I will become through the pain, trauma, and hurt I've endured. For much of my life, I behaved as if everything happening to, within, and around me was okay, and I didn't let anyone in to help me. That was not a healthy way to live. Among the things I've learned is this: Being brave doesn't mean you have to tackle life's challenges alone. It means you have to allow yourself to be vulnerable enough with your feelings to seek help. It's not easy to work through the emotions you deal with when you experience trauma. It's even gut-wrenching at times, but I know that if I do the work and move through my feelings, there is freedom on the other side of pain. And I refuse to give up.

Many therapists and spiritual leaders say we are given experiences in life to teach us lessons. The problem is that we tend to run from pain and seek out pleasure. It takes courage to stay with the pain, heading right into the internal storm instead of stuffing it, avoiding it, or circumventing it. But when I head into the storm with the right people behind me and with the right tools to work with instead of avoiding the pain, I survive every storm I encounter.

I am a survivor. I choose not to be a victim. It is a healthy choice because adapting a victim mindset is avoidance behavior, and it surrenders your power to the people and things that have traumatized you. There are times when I have to tell myself to do the healthy thing, not the victim thing. I still deal with PTSD.

My brother hid his pain and numbed it with drugs and self-destructive behavior. And not only did my mother indulge in self-destructive behavior, she also surrendered her full identity to become the only thing she was comfortable being: a cop's widow. They both adopted a victim's mindset. It is easy to fall into, but it is also deadly.

Have I battled those demons myself? Of course. I've also felt guilty because I didn't know how to help my mother or brother without losing something within me in the process. Among the things I've learned is to take responsibility for myself: my thoughts, my feelings, and my behavior. And I've learned how to forgive. That was the hardest thing for me, but I knew I would not have internal freedom if I did not take back my power and find the courage and love within to forgive.

Years after losing my dad, I had to suffer another huge loss—the ending of my marriage—to realize that I had way more responsibility in relationships than I'd been willing to accept. I had to realize on my own that I could not live my life in fear. Conversations Matt and I had prior to our reconciliation were the hardest conversations I've ever had to have with another person.

I've spent more than half my life on the journey to find the real me. I've spent a lot of time reflecting on the type of wife, mom, sister, daughter, and friend I want to be. I've worked hard to find forgiveness for people who hurt me. During my divorce, I learned that some people will not grow with you. I chose to leave those people behind. They were a part of my life for a season and a reason. I've learned that sometimes when I'm trying to do the right things, I might be on an island alone.

I am becoming the woman I want to be. I have not allowed the patterns of abuse I experienced to continue through me as a parent. I have chosen to change the internal conversations I have with myself. Living with depression and anxiety at times has taught me to give myself grace. At times I've had to take baby steps to get past *myself* to move through the pain of my past. That has involved being brave enough to look fear in the face and do the scary stuff. I've done it because I've always been pulled by something bigger than me.

Not everyone will be given the lessons I've been given and not everyone will grow when they are given these lessons.

But my hope is that I can navigate my life well, learn from my mistakes, accept and successfully work through the lessons I encounter, and help others in the process.

20

Another Step Toward Healing

During my grief journey, I never wanted to attend another law enforcement funeral. But when I heard that an Aurora, Colorado, detective had been gunned down in his car and that he had a teenage daughter, I felt connected somehow and was compelled to attend his funeral.

I knew attending the funeral was going to be difficult and a very hard step to take. I called my mom to tell her I was attending. She sounded disappointed for some reason, but she immediately reminded me to wear a blue ribbon pinned to my clothes. I felt a little indifferent about it, but I wore it anyway. The day wasn't about my story. It was about the family from Aurora. I felt connected to the daughter of the slain cop, even though we'd never met. She and I were part of a horrible club I would never wish on anyone: the children of murdered cops.

As I drove to the Denver church where the service was to be held, I felt a lump in my throat. I had to walk about half a mile from where I parked to the church, and I saw rows of police vehicles lining the street. Trying to gather my thoughts, I felt the familiar tingling in my fingertips and began to sweat. I told myself to breathe.

Officers were on both sides of the street as I approached the church, and my heart began to pound. I wanted to run away, but I told myself that this detective's daughter needed me to be there for her, even if she never knew I was there. I *wanted* to be there. I *had* to be there.

At the stairs leading to the church doors, I was stopped by a female police officer. She had noticed the blue ribbon on my lapel. "Are you a police survivor?" she asked.

I was taken aback. "Yes, I'm a police survivor," I replied.

"Here in Denver?"

"No. I'm an LAPD police survivor."

"Wait here," she said.

I stood there wondering what was happening. "Come with me," she said when she returned.

She led me through the middle aisle up to the front section of the church. I thought she had made a mistake because she sat me behind the mayor of Denver and all the Denver area law enforcement leadership. It was a way of showing respect for a family member of a fallen police officer, but I was uncomfortable among the police leadership. I listened to the priest eulogize the detective. I listened to his colleagues tell funny stories. I kept my emotions in check, knowing that everything I was experiencing was helping me get stronger in my healing.

I kept thinking about his daughter as she sat in the pew listening to the kinds of things I'd listened to at my dad's funeral.

She would have her own journey, and I hoped she would not live her life in victimhood. I hoped she would find the right people to help her navigate her pain. I learned that the detective also had a son, and I hoped he didn't feel left out and unimportant as I had.

As they drove away from the church after the service, I felt I had made a giant leap toward my healing. I sat in my car and wept, wishing my mother and brother could have felt the healing emotions I was feeling. PTSD had taken so much from all of us. For years, none of us knew how to navigate our emotions in a healthy way. For years, my days had felt empty. I never knew what my mom was feeling because she never let me in, even as an adult. I'd watched my brother go down the wrong road, and I'd wanted to protect him but didn't know how.

It saddened me every day that I was unable to have a relationship with my brother because of his self-destructive behavior. I had to create boundaries for the sake of my own mental wellness, but watching my brother destroy his life with drugs was excruciating. My mother had enabled him and made excuses for his behavior, and while I knew that was dysfunctional, I also knew I didn't understand what it was like to be a mother whose kid was spiraling down as he was. I knew she was trying to do the best she could, just as she had when my dad, the love of her life, was killed. My relationships with my mom and my brother had taught me lessons in forgiveness as well as lessons about setting boundaries and developing relationships that encouraged me to be a better person.

I was continuing to heal, and I knew it would likely be a lifelong process.

21

Finding My Tribe

I'd often read and heard that we should surround ourselves with the kind of people we want to grow into. At forty, I decided it was time to shift my career and my mindset.

In 2008, my hairstyling business was struggling, just as the rest of the economy was struggling. I felt stuck in my career, and I wanted something more, something different, but I didn't know what that was. A client of mine was a Realtor® who had helped us sell one home and buy another. She was vivacious, funny, and compassionate—all the things I strived to be.

When I first met Beckie at the salon, her hair didn't fit her personality, and I told her I would love to give her a hairstyle that did. Fortunately, she agreed, and I gave her a cute, spunky short style and colored her hair a bright shade of red that brought out her beautiful blue eyes. She continued to see me in the months following that first appointment. One day we talked about her business as she sat in my chair. She seemed upset because she had just fired her assistant that day.

"That's not good," I said.

"She wasn't a good fit," Beckie replied. "Do you know anyone who might be interested in a part-time job?"

I stared at her for a bit in the mirror, took a deep breath, and said, "Yes, I do. I might be interested."

A look of surprise came over her face. "Are you kidding?" she asked, laughing.

"No, I'm not kidding. My business has slowed down and I need some extra cash."

"You're hired!" she exclaimed.

As she left the salon, I wondered what I'd just done. I knew nothing about real estate. But sometimes you have to rely on fate and take a chance, so that's what I did. I followed where the universe was directing me—which was toward something exciting. Even though my training was by trial and error, I caught on quickly. I worked with Beckie and others in the office, and by the spring of 2009, I was ready to take the full plunge into the real estate world and get my license. It took some time because it had been many years since I'd been in school. I failed the test and tried again. I failed again and tried one more time. I wasn't about to quit. I passed the state test on the third try.

I continued to work for Beckie while also learning from other agents and eventually went to work for Keller Williams Realty, a company whose philosophy aligned with mine. I'd needed to find something that felt bigger than me and knew how important having a positive mindset was. Keller Williams taught me to reprogram my brain from all of the negative self-talk of the past into positive self-talk. I felt at home surrounded by like-minded people, and I learned to dream big, which was something I hadn't learned how to do before then. I realized the company and the people in it were my tribe.

I attended trainings that helped me grow and heal further. Among other things, I learned about creating harmony between my business and personal lives so I could live life by design instead of by default. That was huge for me because after my dad died, I'd lived life by default, doing what I thought was expected of me and trying to please others instead of standing up for the things I believed in.

I was grateful to Beckie for leading me to the path of becoming an owner of a real estate business. I'd never understood the importance of investing in myself, but I was beginning to. I'd moved out of my comfort zone and discovered the leader within myself.

Through a Keller Williams program, I found a coach, Kimberly, who helped me unearth some of my patterns and understand why I'd felt stifled for so long. During a very intense first coaching session, I told Kimberly about the trauma I'd dealt with and how alone I'd felt, even though some people reached out to help me. I admitted that I'd told myself it was my problem, not theirs, and I could handle it without help.

Kimberly listened intently until I finished. "Susan, do you believe in your heart that no one was there to help you?" she finally asked. "Or is it that you refused to allow those people to help you? If so, in doing that, you were putting yourself in a victim mindset by telling yourself you had to do it alone. That mindset is a scarcity mindset."

I needed to find the strength within myself to allow people to help when it was needed. My pattern of insisting on doing it all myself needed to be broken. My first homework assignment before our next call was to choose five people I had not allowed to help me and give them a call. I was to discuss the situation in which I hadn't allowed them to help me, ask for forgiveness, and ask them to hold me accountable if they saw that behavioral pattern in our interactions.

"Ouch!" I exclaimed. She was definitely asking me to step out of my comfort zone for my own benefit. I appreciated it and knew that part of my healing was recognizing my dysfunctional behavioral patterns and changing them. "Okay. I'll think of five people who fit the bill and call them."

As I chose each person, some of them professional relationships and some of them personal relationships, I realized that by not accepting their help, I'd risked making them feel helpless and unimportant. I'd thought I was being gracious by not involving them in my pain, but instead, I was alienating them.

One of the people I had a conversation with was my real estate transaction coordinator. I had done a lot of the transactional things in the beginning of my real estate career when it came down to paperwork and keeping tasks on track. Letting go was hard for me, and it was very hard to let her take care of transactional details for me. I always felt like a burden if I asked for help, but I knew she was frustrated with me for not allowing her to help me by doing some of the tasks that were in her scope of work.

When I picked up the phone to have this conversation, I felt nervous about what she would say, but we had a great conversation about letting go. She listened and was very understanding about her role and holding me accountable to not repeating the behavior of taking on everything myself instead of allowing her to do her job by helping me. She assured me that she was there to help with my business and asked that I not hesitate to delegate things to her. It was an honest conversation, and that was refreshing.

I had conversations with two people connected to my business and three people with whom I had personal relationships. Each conversation taught me a lot about myself.

One of the most life-changing conversations was with Matt. He was the most important person in my life, and I'd been rejecting his help since the beginning of our relationship. I'd made him feel helpless many times because I wouldn't let him play a part in helping me through the deeply painful things I'd felt. It hadn't been fair to him because he was in pain too and probably needed me to be honest with him so we could work it out together. But I'd never recognized *his* pain and had never wanted to put *mine* on him.

As we sat on the living room couch, my body sank into the cushions. I was filled with remorse, and I kept wiping away tears as I asked him for forgiveness for all of the times I had unfairly pushed him aside. He listened intently to every word as if it were the first conversation we'd ever had. Tears welled up in his eyes as he looked into mine. "Thirty-five years together and I'm still learning about you," he said. "Thank you for telling me these things. I love you. I'm here for you always, and I never want you to forget that."

It was the most pivotal conversation in our relationship because I really stepped back and saw everything we had experienced together through a different lens. I realized he'd gone through trauma alongside me, and I'd spent so much time in survival mode myself that I hadn't recognized his pain. He'd been nineteen when my dad died, and like me, he hadn't had the tools to handle his emotions. He'd spent his life trying to be my hero, but I never allowed him to do that.

We'd spent most of our lives not knowing our internal need for acceptance, and this conversation changed it all. For the first time, we saw each other and recognized each other's journeys.

After that conversation with Matt, I kept thinking about everything our marriage had gone through, and it hit me like a Mack truck: Matt had also incurred trauma when my father died. He hadn't had the emotional tools to handle it, and that might have played a part in the self-destructive behavior that led to his infidelity. He'd wanted a different life. Neither of us knew that different life could be with me. We'd both grown individually, making it possible for us to grow together as a couple.

22

All Things Happen for You, Not to You

During my journey, I kept hearing this phrase in my head: God only gives you what you can handle. It took me a long time to accept those words, but now I believe that no matter what the universe throws at you, you have the choice to learn from it and grow from the experience. I realize it's often not easy. The road is treacherous at times, but for those with PTSD, if you continue to heal from the trauma, the road will eventually get easier.

I still live with the effects of PTSD every day. The difference between how I lived with it for many years and how I live with it today is that I'm now aware of the triggers that send me into anxiety and depression. I'm able to rise up and do what I need to do to get through those days.

When Matt and I reconciled and remarried, I sought out a therapist who specialized in EMDR treatment for PTSD. I was at a point in my healing journey where I could introduce myself to more ways of managing my PTSD, so I made an appointment with a new therapist. I had no expectations about outcome. I didn't want to think of EMDR as a magic pill, even though I'd heard that others had experienced great results with that type of therapy.

When I walked into the therapist's office, I noticed that the room was dimly lit. She explained that she needed to create a relaxing environment and the lack of bright lights helped. I sat on a worn brown leather couch across from her, and she handed me two slender paddles with wires attached to them. This was her preferred technique with clients.

My hands felt a little sweaty as I held the paddles in anticipation of the session. She said that the reactions of people during a session varied and that any emotions I felt would be safe because she would not let me feel out of control.

She began by having me visualize my happy place, which for me was on a beach. I felt the breeze on my face and heard the sound of small waves lapping the sand. I was at peace. She told me to go to that place if I felt emotionally out of control at any time during the session.

Earlier, as I drove to the session, I'd thought about my dad and about letting Matt back into my heart. I wondered if reconciling with Matt had been the right thing to do. And as I sat on her couch, those thoughts returned. My therapist could see the change in my body and knew I had left my happy place. She gently told me to return to the beach, feeling the sun on my face and the ocean breeze.

This time, I wasn't alone at the beach. Both my dad and Matt's dad were standing on a bridge overlooking the beach. They looked deep into my soul and smiled at me, and in that moment, I knew everything Matt and I were doing to repair our relationship was right and that they were both happy about it. It was a lot to take in, but as we started to dive into my trauma, I felt that they were both with me and would protect me on this new journey.

I had only a couple of sessions of EMDR work, but that work did soften some of the intensity I felt when I faced something that might trigger me. Every time there is a mass shooting or an officer is killed, I feel it. I let myself feel the emotions. My first reaction is always sadness. Then anger. Those who don't have PTSD may feel the same things, but the difference between them and me is that every time it happens, I get sent back to the time when I lost my dad. The sights, sounds, and emotions of that time come flooding into my brain. But I don't stay there. I remember my EMDR sessions and visualize my happy place. Usually deep breathing and positive self-talk also help to alleviate the intense emotions and visceral responses I have to the situation.

One of those times was after the mass shooting at a Boulder, Colorado, grocery store. Ten people were killed, and one of them was a police officer. When the news of the shootings broke, I decided that the healthy thing for me to do was to avoid media coverage, so I watched no TV news and paid no attention to social media for a couple of days. The police officer's funeral was the following week, and I also chose not to watch coverage on that because of my triggers. Doing those things made me feel in control of my emotions and in control of choosing healthier ways of handling situations like that shooting.

A couple of days after the police officer's funeral, I headed to our local grocery store, which was in the same chain as the one in the Boulder shooting. As I rolled my cart toward the front of the store, I saw that the employees had created a makeshift memorial board for all the victims of the Boulder shooting. I glanced at it and saw all the faces, including the officer's face.

As I continued shopping, I felt the tingling starting in the tips of my fingers. My stomach began to quiver and I became clammy. I stopped in the middle of the aisle. My heart started pounding as I realized I was going into a full panic attack. People were staring at me, and I bolted to the self-checkout. Feeling like I was coming out of my skin, I paid for the groceries and raced to the car. When I got there, I threw the bags in the back, jumped in the car, and tried to manage my breathing, but it was hard to catch my breath while sobbing.

Right there in the store parking lot, I rolled down the window to feel a slight breeze on my face. I struggled to visualize my beachy happy place as cars whizzed by my window. I managed to concentrate on my breathing as I inhaled and exhaled and felt the pressure on my chest dissipate. My skin temperature slowly returned to normal and the tingly feeling in my fingers lessened. I sat there in my car in total disbelief. I hadn't had that kind of reaction in a very long time, so it threw me.

On the short drive home, I analyzed what had happened and figured out that two things had triggered me: seeing the memorial board and experiencing the old feeling of being in danger.

As I continued to relax that night, a sense of peace came over me. I was grateful to have the tools to help myself in that state of panic. I had moved through the emotions and felt better for it. When I journaled about it the next morning, I felt a huge sense of accomplishment.

Events like that shooting remind me how precious life is. I'm grateful for the relationships I have with my kids and Matt. I've worked to teach my kids that life can throw you some very painful and challenging times, but with the right support, you can get through them. Those lessons have even trickled down to their friends over the years.

During my journey, I've not only been a mom to my biological and bonus kids, but Matt and I have always tried to give all kids the extra support they need. We believe it takes a village. I lived with a parent who abandoned me emotionally at the hardest time in my life, and I want to do what I can to prevent children from feeling as I did. No child should feel alone or unsupported. I've taken all of the lessons I've learned about myself when I was struggling and applied them in relating to others going through their own struggles.

Over the years, we have given love and support to many of our kids' friends. These supportive relationships with kids is our "church." It is our way of loving and of respecting the adage that one should treat others as they wish to be treated.

I've learned so much from these kids about strength and also about my own mental health. I love when they call me Momma Susan. It reminds me that my role in their lives is important to them. They trust me and know I have their back. I hold them accountable and make sure they're safe. Because of my own struggles, I understand the pitfalls of mental illness and I'm able to help support some of the kids who struggle. I try to keep an open mind and speak from love, not anger.

Matt and I have always given my kids' friends a safe place to feel loved unconditionally. We consider ourselves mentor parents. I have often said jokingly that while some people collect tchotchkes, we collect children—and now grandchildren from those grown kids.

One such kid has been my "bonus" daughter, as I've called her since we began our mentor relationship when she was a teen. It was a very trying time for her, and I just tried to give her the support she needed. When we met, she reminded me of myself as a teen. Her relationships with her parents were a struggle, she took on a lot, and she didn't feel worthy. I wanted to give her the support I lacked at that age. In supporting kids, I try to help them self-discover what they need in their own journey. And I try to assure them that they don't have to make that journey alone—one of the biggest lessons I have learned on my own journey. Just as others helped me on my journey, I'm committed to helping others on theirs.

In my own journey, I searched out and discovered what would be integral to my recovery. That included people, practices, mind sets, and strategies. I try to assure others I meet in trauma recovery that the reward for doing the work is great. It is reclaiming your power and your life. One lesson of trauma recovery is to do the hard work. PTSD affects people in different ways. For some people, myself included, it causes anxiety or depression. For some, personality disorders, ADHD, or bipolar disorder can stem from PTSD. And these disorders can be stacked on top of each other. I've learned to live with anxiety and help myself through depression. I've learned to be honest with myself when I'm having an emotion-filled day and to allow myself to feel those emotions instead of hiding from them. I've learned to forgive and I've learned how to live in the present instead of the past. I could not have developed those understandings and abilities without the help I've received from therapy.

I still get triggered, but I now recognize those triggers and move through my emotions with the treatment modalities I've learned. One of those modalities is allowing myself to move through anxiety using breathing techniques. Visualization (what I call going to my happy place) is another important tool. I also journal and have found it a powerful way to impact my mindset. I like to journal everything I'm grateful for. It reminds me that no matter what is going on around me at that moment, there are also good things in my life.

Surrounding myself with people who are positive and who support me has also been important. But it is not just a supportive ear or good counsel that is helpful, it is also the positive interactions and conversations I have with these people.

Ultimately, it isn't what life throws at us, it's how we deal with it and what we learn from it that is important. Challenges can take us down or they can inspire us to rise up. And when we rise up, grow more into our true selves, and live more fully, the challenges have not simply happened *to* us, they have happened *for* us and for our benefit. Many years ago, I chose to not let all of the trauma and pain keep me from the life I dreamed of creating.

23

Rose-Colored Glasses

Before all my self-discovery and mindset work, I felt I lived someone else's life. Everything I saw was a half-truth about reality. Part of that was due to my lack of self-worth. I didn't want to see the full truth in things, so I made excuses for how I saw things. That lead to my inability to accept people for who they truly are instead of the fantasy of who I wanted them to be.

This was unearthed when I took a look at my relationships. I had a fantasy about who I wanted my mother to be for me. I've let that go to accept the person she is. I can't even imagine what she felt when her world was flipped upside down. And she had two children to deal with too. But I now recognize that she did the best she could with the situation. As for my brother, it was hard watching him spiral down into the abyss of drug use and self-destructive behavior. I dreamt of a day when he would get clean and have the life he deserves. I had to recognize that he had probably dealt with survivor's guilt and lack of self-worth, and I had spent so much time in fight, flight, or freeze that it was hard for me to be the sister he needed growing up.

I needed to get past my expectations about how I wanted my relationships to be, but before I could do that, I needed to hold myself accountable for some of the mistakes I'd made. My dad had taught me about expectations and accountability and how it can change how you deal with life. To have true accountability, I had to have some uncomfortable conversations with Matt, my mom, and some friends. My dad always spoke the truth, no matter what the outcome. That was difficult for me because I had a history of not wanting to rock the boat and was deeply afraid of the possible outcomes stemming from those conversations.

"You can't look at life through rose-colored glasses all the time because if you do, you'll be missing the important lessons in life," he'd said to me. He had to see reality every day at work, and he wanted me to develop the ability to see and acknowledge life realistically.

I'm human, I fail, and I'm damaged. I acknowledge that about myself, but the failures and my damaged self are not all that defines me. To tell my story, I had to keep stepping out of my comfort zone. I had to be brave enough to own my story and tell it. I now talk about my experiences through a clear lens, a lens that shows me a life full of anticipation and not expectation. It shows me the truth and not just the truth I made up in my mind. Now I tell my story from strength and self-awareness—a strength I feel within myself when I walk my path of healing.

24

What Would Dad Do?

Since my dad's death, along with depression and anxiety, I've struggled with situations that cause me anger. When that happens, my rule has been to ask myself what my dad would do. He dealt with a lot of situations in which he could have lost it, but he never did. There have been many times when I could have lost it too but didn't.

One night when I was a teen, I was nestled in my bed for the night and my parents were in the living room watching television when I heard a loud screech and impact. I sprang from my bed and heard my dad open the door and run outside. I watched from a window and saw our bright yellow Fiat smashed and on the other side of the street, facing the wrong way. My dad was yelling at a man who was walking around his car. I could tell by my dad's body language that he was extremely angry.

From what I could hear, the man was extremely intoxicated. My dad asked him where he thought he was, and the man kept saying he was at the airport. Dad told him he was an hour away from the airport and interrogated him, maintaining his cool as he did. Some neighbors came out of their houses to see what was going on, and Dad explained to the man that he was a law enforcement officer. The guy went to his trunk and pleaded for my dad and the neighbors to take his beer. He seemed to be trying to *bribe* them with beer.

Dad told him he was going to jail. I watched as my dad continued to keep his anger in check. The local police arrived and hauled the guy away in handcuffs.

I was stunned that my dad didn't do damage to the *guy* for all the damage he did to the *Fiat*, but of course, it wouldn't have been like him to do that. I knew in my heart that he was more interested in protecting his family and others by getting this guy off the streets. That night, I realized I could be just like my dad. He was human and had an angry response to the situation, but instead of becoming out of hand, he handled it with integrity. That was a big lesson for me as a teenager, and his handling of that incident still reminds me to always handle my anger with integrity. It's easy to get swept up in the emotions of a situation, but I've learned to keep grounded, and I believe it has come from seeing my dad model that behavior.

My dad was hunted down and killed because of his job, and sadly, many more have followed him. Every time I see a story of another fallen officer, I lament that this needs to stop. I get angry. I think of the police officer's family and their loss. But I don't let that anger envelope me anymore. I know my dad saw death, depravity, and other things on the job that would make anyone angry or depressed. I can't imagine the toll it took on his mental well-being. PTSD is a real thing for those in law enforcement, but my dad told me there was a stigma against officers getting professional help, and that needed to change.

When I was just a baby and my dad was a patrol officer, he got a call one day to go to a home where a woman was high on PCP. She had an infant and was stomping on it because she thought it was possessed by the devil. It took multiple officers to subdue her. My dad immediately scooped the baby up and rushed it to the hospital. Considering that *he* had an infant daughter at home, I can't imagine the emotions he was feeling. My mom said he came home and immediately scooped me up in his arms.

I'm sure the incident traumatized him, but at that time, there was no encouragement for officers to talk through the things they dealt with and few resources for them if they'd wanted to. Some turned to drugs, drinking, or infidelity to deal with things. My dad did the opposite. Every day, he came home grateful for his family. Instead of seeing the worst in people and bringing that home, he left his work at work, to the extent that was possible, and focused on the the things in life that brought him joy when he came home.

Unfortunately, doing that meant he compartmentalized what he experienced in his work without having the tools to work through the trauma he experienced. I found myself doing the same thing for many years until I came to understand how unhealthy it was to avoid my emotions.

Learning to allow myself to feel emotions and not shut them down when things got difficult was one of the most important skills I had to develop. I've made self-care a priority, and whenever a wave of grief washes over me, as it still sometimes does, I remind myself that I need to step back and take care of myself first because I cannot take care of others if I haven't done that.

My dad never lost it when he faced difficult situations, and I've not only emulated that, I've tried to model it for my kids and teach them healthier, more humane ways of dealing with life's problems than losing it—and without stuffing emotions. Unfortunately, my dad didn't have the tools I have developed to deal with trauma, but he did live his life in a way that focused on the positive instead of the negative. And when I'm tempted to look at things from a negative standpoint, I ask myself what my dad would do.

This is one of his legacies, and if I have modeled that outlook well enough for my children, the legacy will continue, with the addition of managing instead of just compartmentalizing emotions. My hope is that as adults, my kids will ask themselves, "What would Mom do?"

25

The Legacy

Through the years, I've watched the ripple effect of every traumatic experience I've had chip away at the core of my soul. I've had to peel away the parts that are detrimental to my journey toward resiliency. Every step has been taken with careful consideration. I journal on the days I feel overwhelmed or anxious. When things are too much, I no longer compartmentalize them. I'm accepting of support. I'm able to look in the mirror for the first time in my life and love the person I've become.

With all of the work I've done, my priority has been to be able to help my boys too. My two oldest boys have really taught me a lot about myself. They have watched their mom struggle, and I've watched them both struggle with mental health issues. Dealing with my own mental wellness has helped me understand theirs. I've always told them and the kids I mentor that mental health should be a priority.

There is still a great deal of stigma attached to mental disorders. I have taken offense when people label others as broken.

And during my journey, some people have told me to just get over the depression I suffered. Of course, that's not easy when your body is causing a chemical imbalance in your brain due to trauma. It's not just a matter of feeling sad.

There is so much in play when it comes to understanding mental health issues. My first therapist never discussed depression with me. I didn't learn anything about depression until my breakdown with the Columbine shooting in 1999. Since then, I've learned a great deal about how the brain is affected by trauma. I have extensive memory loss of the time right after my dad was killed. Writing about my journey has helped me uncover some of the memories that were hidden in the back of my brain.

I have moved through many emotions with each step in my journey. The shame and guilt I had for so many years about my relationships with my mother and brother has disappeared. It took many years of hard conversations and peeling away layers of buried issues to get there, but the freedom I feel from doing that work is priceless.

In a strange way, my healing is a part of my dad's legacy. My dad was a remarkable man, and I got to be his daughter, even if it was for a shorter time than I would have wanted. I had seventeen years of his love and advice. That was enough time to instill a strength I didn't know I had, a burning energy I had to learn to channel to do the hard work of dealing with the trauma in my life. My dad instilled a sense of responsibility in me, and one of the ways I embody that is to live my life as he would have wanted me to.

They say that a legacy is the dash between your birth-date and your death date. My dad not only made an incredible impression on friends and family, but also on perfect strangers, including those who heard the story of his heroic last act of love: protecting his son. That act showed his true character and what an amazing man and father he was. My dad inspired boys to grow up to have careers in law enforcement. He was a hero to many. When I think of the legacy I hope to leave, that includes instilling in my boys the desire and ability to be brave regardless of what they experience in life. I want them to feel that they have the strength within to get through anything and that they will be better for it in the end.

I want my boys to continue positive patterns when they become parents: To never talk down to their kids or make them feel they aren't important. To make sure that their mental and physical health are a priority. To understand that a healthy mind is one of the things that creates a healthy body.

I discovered my purpose during my journey, and that purpose started with my dad's death. I believe that everyone is given things to struggle with in life, and how you respond is the key to finding out how resilient you can be.

Legacy is what drives me. I'm working to carry on my dad's legacy by making a positive mark in this world. Helping those on grief and trauma journeys is what I work toward every day. It hasn't been an easy road, but I wouldn't have changed a thing about any of the pain I had to endure through the process. I'm pretty sure I have felt my dad's presence many times over the years reminding me that I'm my father's daughter. I'm honored to carry on his legacy.

Be at peace within yourself. The world changes. Our lives change. And we change with it.

Matt and me (top and bottom)

Acknowledgments

I want to thank all the people in my life who have helped me through this journey. First, I would like to thank my husband. He has been on this journey right alongside me. He has supported me in writing this book and has never wavered in his belief that helping people through my story is my purpose in life.

I would like to thank my wonderful boys who watched their mom learn to grow through the years and supported me through it all.

I want to thank my mom for allowing me to find my own way through my grief journey.

I would like to thank my brother for continuing to love me, even though our lives took different paths.

I want to thank Ronda Courtney, Kris Garrett, my coach, Kimberly Guiry, and all the people who were integral to getting this book out, who believed in my story, and who encouraged me in the writing process. I want to thank my editor, Melanie Mulhall, for encouraging me through the writing process.

It wouldn't have been possible to write this book without all the love and encouragement.

About the Author

Susan Snow is the daughter of LAPD Detective Thomas C. Williams, who was killed in the line of duty on October 31, 1985. She is a successful Realtor® living with her husband, Matt, and her stepson, Daniel, in the Denver suburbs. This book was born out of Susan's journey through the trauma she experienced with the death of her father. She wrote it to heal herself and help others heal through her words and experiences. Susan has appeared in several media outlets and public speaking forums. To learn more about her, visit www.SusanSnowSpeaks.com.

www.ingramcontent.com/pod-product-compliance
Lightning Source LLC
Chambersburg PA
CBHW070704130626
46553CB00005B/1839